The Red-Headed Stepchild: My Struggle to Survive

by

Katie Grimsley

Foreward

This book was written for all of the children that have been victims of child abuse and/or neglect. Some are survivors that grow up to be positive members of society and wonderful parents to their own children. Others take a dark path that leads to them abusing and/or neglecting their own children, thus continuing the vicious cycle. Many have no opportunities in life; they've grown up in foster care and established no lasting relationships. They may choose a life of crime which leads them to jail or prison. Some leave this world before they have a chance to grow up; victims of such heinous abuse that they lose their lives. Every child matters. Their stories matter. I was a victim. I pray that sharing my story is an inspiration to others to take the positive path. It is possible to overcome the things that happened to us. It is possible to be happy. We are worth the love that we didn't receive as children. We *are* worthy. This book is written in memory of my sweet nephew, whose life was taken before his second birthday by his abuser. He has not been forgotten. He was loved. His life mattered.

This book is dedicated to my sister, Emma. We went through our journey together, and without one another, we would not have survived.

The Revelation

Last night, I stood in the darkness of the inflatable tunnel on the football field at my son's high school. Standing close to my side with his arm interlocked in mine was my tall, handsome, athletic, blonde-headed and blue-eyed baby boy. In half an hour, the last home game of his senior year would start. It would be the last time I would get to see him play on that home field. On his other side stood one of my dearest friends, his stepmother. She held tightly to his father's hand, and we all joked with one another as she and I tried to hold back tears. Our baby boy was growing up, and we could not contain our pride in the young man he had become. Somewhere in the stands the rest of our family waited to hear Patrick's name called and see us escort our son onto the field. As I heard Patrick's name, and the announcer listed Patrick's parents' names (all three of us), Patrick squeezed my arm and the four of us walked onto the field. I held my head high and smiled at the crowd, incredibly proud of the young man I was escorting and filled with joy that God chose me to be one of his mothers. The spectators in the stands, with the exception of those that knew me well, had no idea what a dark past I came from. They only saw a proud, happy, confident woman escorting her son on one of the most important days of his life. When I was Patrick's age, my life was quite different. By his age, God had saved me. On a dark night twenty-three years ago, I stood in front of the mirror in my bathroom with tears streaming down my face and a razor blade in my hand. Seventeen years of misery had come to a head and I felt that there was no other way out. I had been miserable from my earliest memories, and I just couldn't take it anymore. As I stood there, I took what I originally thought was one last look at myself. My eyes were swollen and red, my face was streaked with tears, and the sadness was unmistakable. Then I heard something; it was a sound from deep inside my soul. God told my heart that there was more to life than this. The misery that I had experienced for years was not all that this life had to offer me. God told me that I was His child and that He loved me. If I took my own life, He wouldn't allow me into

His kingdom. However, if I trusted in Him, I could find happiness on Earth and eventually eternity with Him. Something inside of me was ready to fight. I had never been a fighter. I had survived years of abuse by hiding, never speaking up, and never drawing attention to myself. I had walked down school hallways with my head down and eyes averted so I wouldn't be noticed, much less interacted with. In that moment, God gave me the strength to become a fighter. He wanted me to live and fulfill His destiny for me. He told me that one day, I would become a mother. I would have the opportunity to bring new life into this world and love my children. In that moment, everything about me changed. I was suddenly a fighter, for children that didn't even exist yet. The years that led up to that fateful night would never be forgotten, but they would be used for good from that moment on. Had God not intervened that night, I would never have become a loving mother escorting her son onto a football field for the last time. Never would I have known the strong tug of maternal love and fierce protectiveness for my children, nor the joy they have filled my heart with every day of their lives. The eighteen years of abuse that I endured, and the decades it took me to heal, molded me into the woman standing close to her son on the football field last night. Those eighteen years hold memories that I want to share now, so any child that is going through what I went through will know that there is light at the end of the tunnel. There is a future worth fighting for, and a joy in life that makes those bad memories go away. The little girl I am going to tell you about is a stranger to me now. But her story needs to be told, for every child like her in the past and the future. She needs to be heard.

Chapter 1
The Early Years

My earliest memory was from when I was about two years old. I remember my mother getting ready for a date. She had a friend over, and they were going on a double date with two young men. Mom and her friend were in the bathroom and the young men were waiting in the living room. The overall mood was jovial as I stood shyly by the door to the living room watching the young men. They laughed and joked around, smiling back at me when I smiled at them. The next memory I have was one of them burning my lip with a lit cigarette and laughing about it. I learned quickly to stay away from them. Within a few months, I was in a hospital following a severe beating. Children's Protective Services removed me from my mother's custody and placed me in foster care. She and my father were divorced and when my father found out where I was, he immediately petitioned the court for custody. I don't remember being in foster care. I don't remember being beaten, and I also don't remember the other things that I found out years later happened to me before my removal. The next thing I remember is being in a day care center telling my friends that my daddy was coming to pick me up when he got off work. I was happy and I was safe. Then my mother came to pick me up. I didn't know what happened to my father, but I remember being in a car with my mother for a long time. She let me lay down with my head on her lap while a strange man drove the car. The strange man was my stepfather and the source of the next 15 years of misery in my life.

After driving for a long time, I was reunited with my older sister, Emma. We were in a trailer house with my mother and the strange man. My mother told us that he was our stepfather and he introduced himself to us. He smiled a lot and made a big deal about how excited he was that we were there. I had already learned from the last time that strange men with big smiles weren't good. They weren't safe and they would hurt me. I wanted to be with my father. I asked where he was and never got a straight answer. I was told that my stepfather was my father now. We stayed in that trailer for a long time. A man came to visit me there. He always wanted to see me and always asked if I was okay. I told him I was because I was three years old and didn't know how to tell him anything different. My heart cried out for my father every day. I would lay in my bed in the strange new house with the strange new father and listen to my sister's breathing in the bed next to me. I cried quietly for my father, hoping that somehow he would hear me from wherever he was and come get me. I wanted nothing more in life but for him to show up at the door and take me away with him. Over and over I would squeeze my eyes tightly shut and try to remember my father's face. I didn't want to forget what he looked like. I would wish upon a star each night before bed that when I woke up the next morning, he would be there. He never was. My mother didn't take me to church and I didn't know about God. I didn't know that I could pray to Him. I was a tiny, lonely, sad little girl wishing as hard as I could that my father would come for me. He never did. Sometimes my mother and I would ride into town in her car together. I would sit in the back seat and watch the buildings whiz by. One day, I saw a building that reminded me of my father! It was big and looked like the top of a soccer ball. I knew my father was somewhere close to that building! I got so excited and asked my mother to take me to that building to see my father. She got upset and told me that my father wasn't there and never had been. Years later I discovered that the building in question was a water treatment plant just inside the military base that my father was stationed at. It could be seen from the road by the gate to the base, and was indeed where my father had been at one point.

My early years were spent in South Dakota. This is where Children's Protective Services removed me and where I ended up living with my mother and stepfather after reunification. My mother had married a man ten years her senior. He had three children of his own; all of them were older than me. I was the youngest out of five children, and our home was chaos when my step-siblings came to visit in the summers. There were new rules to follow and I had to adjust to a whole new life. The one person I could depend on, who always tried to look out for me, was Emma. She and I stuck together like glue, especially when our step-siblings were around. We soon realized that we were second-class citizens in our new home, and that we were unwanted. The man that came to ask if I was okay kept coming. Before he came, our mother and stepfather would sit Emma and I down and tell us what to say when the man came. I didn't realize we were being coached to tell the man that everything was fine. I wanted to be a good little girl and I did as I was told.

My stepfather started off with smiles and assertions that he was happy to be our stepfather. Unfortunately, his actions stated differently. We had lived with him for a short time when my sister and I were eating supper one night. He did not like how quickly we were eating and came up behind us without us realizing he was there. He knocked both of our chairs over, causing us to fall backwards onto the ground. Then he yelled at us for several minutes because of the mess we made knocking our plates over when we fell. Our mother sat in the living room and didn't say a word. I believe she was shocked that he did that, and didn't know how to react. Our chairs were picked up and as our stepfather screamed at us, we tried to clean up the mess. I began to cry because I was scared and he screamed even louder. I fought back my tears and tried to compose myself so he would stop. I was only three years old. Once the mess was cleaned up, we were told to go to our rooms. We were not allowed to eat because, somehow, everything was our fault. The next time we went to the table to eat, we ate slowly. We didn't want to find ourselves on the ground again, trying to clean up food that went flying off our plates. Unfortunately, that wasn't the right solution because then we got into trouble for eating too slowly. Thus began a life of never being able to do anything right.

Our step-siblings came to visit for the summer when I was about four years old. By this time we had moved from the little trailer to a tiny pink house with a basement. Emma and I quickly learned that there was one set of rules for us and another for them. They were allowed to do just about anything they wanted. We were not allowed to do anything. Emma and I were not supposed to call attention to ourselves or ask for anything. One day, we were all playing in the basement of our tiny house. My stepsister read a book to me. I think it was a Sesame Street book and in the book, a string was tied around a finger so something would not be forgotten. Being four, I thought this was a great idea! I decided I would tie a string around my finger so I wouldn't forget to be quiet. I found a tiny little string hanging from a piece of clothing and tied it around my finger nice and tight. I was so proud of myself; now every time I looked at that little string I would remember to be quiet. If I was quiet, I wouldn't be screamed at. Unfortunately, I didn't realize that the string would cut off circulation in my finger and cause it to become painful and red. As my finger started to throb, I decided maybe it was best to take the string off. I started to tug on it, but it wouldn't budge. As I started to panic, I tried to untie it. I had done a great job tying it nice and tight. The knot wasn't coming out. Emma realized something was wrong and came over to me. She tried to get the string off to no avail. With tears in my eyes, I went to the top of the basement stairs and called out for my mother. We weren't supposed to just go into the main part of the house. We had to ask for permission. My mother and stepfather were making supper. As soon as I called out for my mother, my stepfather became angry. He yanked the door open and yanked me into the kitchen by my arm. "What do you want?!" he yelled at me. I tried to hold back the tears in my eyes and held up my finger. By this time, it was bright red and the throbbing had intensified. "How in the Hell did you do that, you stupid little brat?" he yelled at me. My mother, who was standing in front of the oven, walked over to try to intervene. As soon as she tried to step between us, he sneered at her and pushed her back. "I'll deal with the little brat! Just cook supper!" he yelled at her. He stepped away from me and started rummaging through drawers in the kitchen. As he moved from drawer to drawer, he would slam the drawer he just looked through and sigh loudly. Even at the age of four, I realized he was just getting angrier by the second. I tried to desperately to remove the string myself before he turned around. I was not successful and seconds later, he had located scissors and stomped back over to me. "Sit your ass down!" he yelled at me, pulling a chair out from the table. I sat down quietly, trying hard to hold back my tears, and held my finger out. He roughly grabbed my chubby little hand, yanking it toward him, and quickly cut through the string on my finger. The relief from the pain was short lived. As soon as I stood up to try to shrink back down to the basement, he grabbed me and shook me. I looked up at him and he yelled at me, "Don't ever do something so stupid again, understand?" I nodded and said "Yes, sir." If I didn't realize it before, I realized that day it was incredibly important not to make my existence known and not to ask for help with anything.

A few weeks after the incident with the string on my finger, I woke up in the middle of the night. I had a horrible nightmare and I was crying and trembling. I had dreamt that my father had come to the house to take me home with him, but my stepfather wouldn't let me go. In my dream, I cried out to my father to take me with him as he drove away and my stepfather yelled at me to shut up or he would give me something to cry about. As I lay in my bed trembling, I wanted nothing more than to be able to crawl into bed with my father and have him wrap his arms around me. I wanted to wake up and be at the end of this horrible nightmare that was my reality. I chose the next best thing, my mother. Cautiously, I walked down the hallway in our home. It was silent, dark, and scary. When I reached my mother's room, I hoped that I could see which side of the bed my mother was on. If I was really quiet, perhaps I could wake her up without waking him up. I went to the side of the bed closest to the door and stood there, trying to push away the darkness in the room to see if my mother was there. Suddenly, I was yanked up by a strong arm and turned over. My stepfather had an iron grip on me as he started hitting my bottom. I began to cry as he hit me over and over. "What the Hell are you doing in here? Don't you know what time it is?" he yelled as he continued to hit me. Then he set me down roughly. "Get your stupid ass to bed now and don't you ever wake me up again!" he yelled as I ran quickly from the room. I went straight to my bed and pulled the covers over my head, trying to hide as well as I could. As I laid there, I cried as quietly. Why didn't my father just come get me? I knew he wanted me. He told me he loved me. Did he even know where I was? I laid there for a long time, my eyes closed as tightly as I could, willing away the reality of my situation and hoping that when I woke up in the morning, my father would be there. I cried myself to sleep that night and when I woke up the next morning, my father was not there. Emma was there, though. That was the day that I decided that as long as Emma was there, I would be there. She was my salvation and my reason for being there. She was all I had in the whole world.

When we still lived in the pink house with the basement, I woke up sick one night. It wasn't long after I had been hit multiple times for trying to wake my mother after a nightmare. I was about four or five years old at the time. It was dark and quiet in the house, and I knew that meant my mother and stepfather were already asleep. My stomach rolled, and I knew I needed to throw up. I laid as flat as I could and tried not to move, hoping that the nausea would go away. It didn't. The longer I laid there, the worse it got. I couldn't call out for my mother, because that would wake up my stepfather. I was too sick to handle a beating. If I got out of bed and opened my bedroom door, I risked waking them up and being beaten. Quietly, I got out of bed and tried to find something that I could use. As soon as I stood up, the nausea became overwhelming. I felt something soft at my feet and realized there was a towel on the ground. As I reached down to pick up the towel, I began to vomit. Fortunately, nothing got on the floor. I made it down to my knees and continued to vomit. My whole body shook out of fear of being discovered and being sick. When I finally stopped,

I stayed there for a few moments. On my knees, in the dark, by myself. I rolled up the towel and placed it in the bottom of my closet, hoping it wouldn't be discovered. I climbed back into bed, my heart beating in my ears, as I tried to listen for any sounds of movement in the house. If there was movement, it meant that I had been too loud and woke them up. There was no sound and I breathed a sigh of relief. Eventually, I went back to sleep. When I woke up the next morning, it was time to gather laundry. I gathered my clothes and the dirty towel and walked carefully to the laundry room. As I walked down the hall, I hoped earnestly with every step that the mess I made in the towel would not be discovered. If I was lucky, my mother would be at the washing machine. As I rounded the corner, I realized my stepfather was waiting impatiently by the washing machine with the water already running into it. He was tapping his foot and had a mean look on his face. I tried not to make eye contact with him as I handed over my bundle of laundry. To my relief, he didn't go through it at all and just threw it into the washing machine. My secret was safe. At four or five years old,

I had learned how to cover up being sick and needing help. I had learned how to take care of myself, and I hadn't even started Kindergarten.

We lived in South Dakota when I did start Kindergarten. Emma was a year older than me, so she had started the year before I did. I was excited to get out of the house every day and walk to our little school about a block away. Emma and I went to a private Catholic school. At the time, I didn't realize there was a reason behind our attendance there. If we were in a public school, our father could find us. While attending a private school, our records were kept private and he couldn't find us. It was around this time that my mother and stepfather started talking about terminating my father's rights and my stepfather adopting me. I didn't know what they were talking about. All I knew was that they planned to add my stepfather's name after my current last name with a hyphen between the two. I didn't want my stepfather's name. I only wanted my father's name. One day, I was sitting in class and we had a substitute teacher. I hadn't been able to talk about my name being changed and had been holding all of my thoughts in. The substitute realized something was bothering me and came over to sit by me where I was quietly playing by myself. She chatted with me a little bit and when I felt comfortable, I began chatting back. Finally, I spilled what was bothering me. My father's name was all I had left of him and I didn't want to lose that. The substitute teacher gently patted my hand and assured me that all would be well. Sometimes parents got divorced and kids got new parents, she explained. I didn't want a new parent, I just wanted my father. That day was the first time in a long time that another adult had shown concern for my feelings. I cherished that simple patting of my hand. It gave me a tiny inkling of hope that someday, I would be worth loving.

At home, things continued to get worse. It seemed like the more power my stepfather felt he had, the more we paid for it. We were still going to the private Catholic school and we learned the prayers of the rosary and went to confession each week. I didn't really understand it all since I was so little. When I went to confession, I always tried to confess everything I had done the week prior. Somehow, I knew not to say anything about the things that were happening at home. We weren't supposed to talk about what happened at home; in fact, we really weren't supposed to talk at all. When our stepfather realized my sister and I had memorized the prayers for the rosary, he used that against us. If we misbehaved, we would have to kneel in a corner, facing the wall, with our knees on bags of dry beans. As we knelt, we would have to say the prayers of the rosary. Still, I didn't really know about God and how He could help me. I only knew how to recite the prayers I had been taught. Emma and I would kneel and pray for hours, our knees screaming in pain due to the dry beans poking into the sensitive skin. It was torture for us. I was in Kindergarten and Emma was in first grade. It was better than him hitting us, though. As I knelt there, sometimes I was able to transport myself to a completely different place. I would imagine I was in another world. It was a world where little girls were loved. We weren't burdens. We weren't stupid. My favorite prayer was the Hail Mary. I remember pondering how she was full of grace, and what that really meant. Did she love her child? Was he really the fruit of her womb? What did that really mean? While my stepfather's intent was to punish us and make us feel worthless, he was unintentionally developing my little mind. Perhaps Mary loved all children. Perhaps we were all worthy of love. Perhaps there was a world different from the one I was living in. Maybe somewhere there was a little girl who had a stepfather who loved her and she was sitting on the furniture in the living room, instead of in a lonely little corner kneeling on dry beans because she picked her cup up at dinner with one hand instead of two hands.

Manners were extremely important to our stepfather. We were not allowed to place our elbows on the table. We were not allowed to lean forward as we ate. Instead, we were expected to sit up perfectly straight at all times, and bring the fork to our mouths. We were not allowed to speak at the table.

If we were in public and someone came up to speak to us, we were not allowed to respond. If we wanted to take a drink out of our cup, we were to pick our cup up with two hands. We were not allowed to mix our food up or play with it in any way whatsoever. We were not allowed to eat too fast, nor were we allowed to eat too slowly. Additionally, we were always expected to eat everything on our plate. If we were sick, we were still expected to eat. If we didn't like something, we still had to eat it. If we liked something a little too much, our stepfather made sure he didn't serve it in the future. If we were sick and threw up after supper, we were in trouble for wasting food. If we broke any of the numerous rules at the dinner table, we were punished. It might be a slap to the back of the head. He might pull our hair to the point that he pulled it out. He might take us to our rooms, pull our pants down, and hit us as hard as he could. We never knew what the punishment would be, but we always knew that it would be swift and harsh. It took me years once I was grown to learn to pick up my cup with one hand instead of two.

Our step-siblings came to see us several times when we lived in South Dakota. They lived in Seattle so it wasn't terribly far for them to travel. Ours was a love/hate relationship. The rules were different for *his* kids because he actually loved them. They could get away with a lot of things that we couldn't. If we were out somewhere, they were allowed to speak. Eating at the table, they were allowed to talk quietly. They could actually ask for what they wanted at a restaurant, while our meals were chosen for us. Early on, we learned that they were much more important than we were. Unfortunately for one of our stepbrothers, the rule about eating everything on one's plate applied to him as well. We had cold cereal with milk for breakfast one morning. He didn't like the cereal because we always had Cheerios. Emma and I were not allowed to have sugar because our mother was terrified of us becoming diabetic. Our stepbrother wanted sugar on his cereal and was not allowed to have it. He refused to eat the cereal. As a result, he wasn't allowed to leave the table until he ate every bite. Lunch time came and he was still at the table with the same bowl of cereal. By this time, it was soggy and the milk was warm. He continued to sit at the table, refusing to eat the cereal. It was hamburger night, which was a favorite at our house. As the rest of us sat at the table, eating our hamburgers, he sat in front of the sad little bowl of cereal. It was more mush than anything by this time, with the cereal having soaked up the majority of the milk. Still, he refused to eat it. Finally, bed time came and the cereal was still there. By this time, our stepfather had lost his temper and he took our stepbrother to his room. We heard the belt hitting our stepbrother and him crying. Then he was sent to bed. The cereal was thrown away. The next morning, he got to eat the cereal that he liked. Emma and I were stuck with our Cheerios.

During our time in South Dakota, Emma and I went to a babysitter. We didn't go there for long. The babysitter was an older lady. She had a husband, a son, and a dog. She watched us, her own son, and a couple more children. Her house had a basement and she stuck us all down there. Her son seemed scared all the time and she and her husband screamed at each other a lot. Her husband had a plastic or plaster model of a hand that he told us he cut off of a man that he killed. He scared us and we were happy to be in the basement away from him. The lady didn't like any of us and sent us down to the basement to pick up dog poop. We had to pick it up with our bare hands. I didn't like the basement, but I also didn't like being in the main part of the house with the lady and her husband. One day, I really needed to use the bathroom. I went to the door of the basement and knocked. She didn't come to the door, and it was locked. All of us kids were locked in the basement. I began to panic. I really needed to go to the bathroom right then! I banged and banged on the door, and she still didn't come. Finally, I couldn't hold it anymore and I wet my pants. I sat on the top step, crying, and soaked with urine. The lady finally opened the door. When she saw me sitting there, soaking wet, she yanked me up and spanked me. Then she made me sit on the sofa in the living room, on a plastic bag, until my mother came to pick me up. I sat there for what seemed like hours and finally my mother walked in. I just knew I was going to be in big trouble. My mother asked why I was sitting on the couch and why I hadn't been changed. The lady told her that if I wet my pants, I could just sit in it. Then she told my mother that she spanked me. My mother was livid. For once, I wasn't in trouble. My mother yelled at that lady, telling her that she couldn't treat children that way, and told her that Emma and I wouldn't be back. Then she gathered me and my sister and loaded us up in the car. We never returned. I just knew that I would be in trouble with my stepfather but when we got in the car, my mother fussed the whole way home. He didn't get a chance to get a word in edgewise and for once, I wasn't in trouble with him. That was the one time I remember my mother really standing up for me.

We only lived in South Dakota for a few years. Our stepfather was in the military and it wasn't long before he got orders to report to a new duty station. While in South Dakota, we didn't see our extended family. There were some fun times, but I was little and don't remember much. Once, we went to Mount Rushmore. Our stepfather enjoyed baseball so we spent some time at the baseball fields. There were also cook-outs with military co-workers and their families. In public, our stepfather was on his best behavior and tried to look like the doting dad. We knew that if we misbehaved in public, we would pay for it at home. We were all careful about how we presented ourselves in public, and looked like one happy little family to outsiders. Emma and I knew the truth about home, though. Unfortunately, we had no idea that it was only going to get worse. The more our stepfather got away with, the more he tried over the next several years.

Chapter 2

New Mexico

When we lived in New Mexico, our stepfather was a military recruiter. It wasn't long before he received orders to move to his next duty station, which was in New Mexico. I was in first or second grade at the time, and I learned about the pain of moving and leaving friends behind. However, my sadness was quickly replaced with happiness when I found out we would just be a few short hours from our grandparents. Our grandparents lived in Oklahoma, and it was close enough to visit them or for them to come and visit us. With this possibility came the realization that my grandparents would see how we were being treated and put a stop to it. They had always been good to us, and I knew when my grandmothers found out what had been going on, they would set my stepfather straight. It wasn't long after we moved to New Mexico that we were taught an important new lesson. We weren't allowed to speak about anything that happened in our home. If Emma or I said something as simple as what we had for supper the night before, there would be hell to pay. We had already been taught we weren't allowed to speak unless we were spoken to first. Now, we had to be careful about how to respond. In reality, our stepfather realized that our grandparents would intervene if they found out how he was treating us. He took steps to ensure that didn't happen. He took our voices.

Our step-siblings came to visit very soon after we moved to New Mexico. When they were there, our mother and stepfather got into a horrendous argument. There was lots of screaming and cursing between them. At one point, our stepfather walked out of the house and left in my mother's car. Our stepsister said something snarky to our mother, and our mother slapped her. Then our mother sat at the kitchen table and cried for a long time. It seemed like hours to me, and during that time, our stepfather didn't return. I hid in my room and every few minutes I would peer out the door. At one point, our mother was on the phone with the police saying that she wanted to report her car stolen. Eventually, our stepfather came back and they argued some more. Later that evening, Emma and I were told to tell our step-siblings goodbye because we were leaving with our mother in the morning. I had not been happy in a long time, but that news was the best news I had heard in my entire life. We told our step-siblings goodbye and went to bed. I stayed up for a long time, happy that we were leaving in the morning. Maybe I would get to see my dad again. I finally drifted off to sleep with a smile on my little face and contentment in my heart. The next morning, I woke up ready for the day ahead. My happiness turned to incredible disappointment when I walked out of my room and saw my mother and stepfather cuddling on the couch. They had made up some time during the night. We weren't going anywhere. Instead, we were stuck there with *him*.

Sometime close to Christmas, my maternal grandparents came to visit. They had a small dog that we adored, and they brought him with them. When they arrived, Emma and I were sitting at the table eating our supper. The dining area in our home was adjacent to the kitchen and the living area was on the other side of the kitchen. Emma and I sat at that table for every meal while our mother and stepfather sat in the living room. We never ate together as a family because Emma and I weren't wanted. We were too disgusting to be allowed to eat with our parents and weren't allowed in the living room unless there were special circumstances. When we did eat our meals, we were required to listen for a break in their conversation and then call out for permission to leave the table. There was even a small speech we had to recite, which went: "Mom and Dad, I am sorry to interrupt you. I have finished my meal. May I please be excused from the table?" We had to be very careful that we didn't interrupt them and that what we felt was a break in their conversation was, indeed, a break in their conversation. If we were incorrect and interrupted their conversation, we were in big trouble. On this particular evening, our grandparents and their dog, Skipper, arrived during our meal. Skipper came into the dining area, excited because he hadn't seen us in years. We were not done with our meal. As a result, we were not allowed to pet him or even acknowledge him in any way whatsoever. We also hadn't recited our speech yet, which we weren't allowed to do until we had eaten everything on our plates. Skipper became so upset that he became ill, vomiting on the dining room floor. Our grandmother came into the dining room looking for us, and became upset when she saw that Skipper was ill and we hadn't helped him. She didn't understand that we had to follow the rules, and when our stepfather came into the room, we got into trouble for not acknowledging our grandmother or Skipper. On that night, I realized that we had to follow the rules but in following the rules, we would get into even more trouble if that made our stepfather look bad. We were in a no-win situation and still had over a decade left in that family.

After our grandparents visited us in New Mexico, they took Emma and I back to Oklahoma with them for about a week. We finally got to see our extended family for the first time in years. This included our aunts, uncles, and grandparents from our father's side of the family. As we rode in the car to Oklahoma, I began to recognize the area around our hometown. I got excited because I thought that perhaps I would get to see my father. I couldn't contain my excitement and asked my grandparents, "Are we going to get to see Daddy Darrell?" My grandmother asked me why I called my father 'Daddy Darrell' and I explained that we were told to call our new stepfather

'Dad' and could only refer to our father as 'Daddy Darrell.' It was a rule in our home, and one which we knew not to break. We weren't allowed to ask about our father, and definitely weren't allowed to say that we loved or missed him. Unfortunately for me, I was the spitting image of my father. I was told many times how I was so ugly and my cheeks were so chubby, just like my father. As a result, I began to shy away from people and hide my face. The only difference between my father and I was that my hair had a red tint when it hit light just right. I was the red-headed stepchild; the one that looked like my father and suffered as a result.

    Once we made it to Oklahoma, we had a brief respite from the Hell that was our home back in New Mexico. We saw our paternal grandparents as well as other family on that side. Our Aunt Teresa and Uncle Richard were there. They had not been married long and Emma had been very close to them before our stepfather came into our lives. When Uncle Richard arrived to pick Aunt Teresa up for dates, Emma would look at him with her big blue eyes and ask to go along. He couldn't resist her and always took her with them. Now they were married and starting a family of their own. We knew not to tell anyone that things were not okay at home, but somehow Aunt Teresa knew. We stayed in Oklahoma for about a week, then it was time to go home. Aunt Teresa gave us a few dollars each in coins about half an hour before we made it back to our house. She told us to hide the money in our shoes so it wasn't taken away from us when we got home. I still remember how the coins felt against my little feet, and trying to walk quietly into the house with them so they wouldn't be discovered. When we got to the front door and knocked, our mother came to the door. She kissed each one of us and told us she missed us. I was too worried about the coins in my shoes to even notice. Our stepfather was behind her and told us to come into the living room. We did, and found a huge mess. All of our gifts that we had opened were strewn about along with the packaging. He never told us he missed us or was happy to see us. Instead, he screamed at us for what seemed like forever.

We had left a mess when we left for Oklahoma, and he made sure we knew it. He let us know that he wasn't there to pick up after us, and that we were grounded until he decided otherwise. That's when I realized that grounding us did no good. If we weren't cleaning the house or doing homework, we were banished to our rooms anyway. Sometime during all of the commotion and trying to clean up the mess from the week before, the coins in our shoes were discovered. The money our Aunt Teresa gave to us was confiscated, because stupid little brats like us didn't deserve money. We cost our stepfather too much money as it was, and he was tired of having to pay for everything.

When we lived in New Mexico, I developed an anxiety disorder. I would get horrible stomach aches and go to the nurse's office at school at least once a week. If we traveled to Oklahoma to visit, I would be fine on the trip there. As soon as we got in the car to go home, I would be sick. For the entire drive, I would be sick and have to pull over multiple times to vomit. My mother could never figure out what was wrong with me, but I knew that the closer I got to being home, the closer I was to being hit or screamed at again. If I got sick at school, I wouldn't ask to go home unless I knew it was only my mother at home. She wasn't mean to us. She would kiss us and hug us and tell us she loved us. My mother actually wanted us at home. Our stepfather didn't and he let us know that every chance he got. We still weren't allowed in the living room unless it was a special occasion of some kind. Emma and I spent most of our time in our rooms or in the dining room. Our time in the bathroom was even restricted, and we had to keep the door unlocked at all times. One night, I was feeling a little rebellious and locked the door to the bathroom while I was in the bathtub. We had planned to go to the swimming pool earlier that day and the plans had been cancelled. I had put my bathing suit on underneath my clothes in anticipation of swimming, even though I knew I wasn't supposed to put my bathing suit on without my stepfather's permission. I was still in the bathtub when my stepfather got home. He came to the bathroom to check on me and tried to open the door. When he realized the door was locked, he became extremely angry and started pounding on the door. I jumped out of the tub, naked, to open the door. As soon as I unlocked the door, he threw it open and started screaming at me for locking it. He glanced over at the pile of my clothes in the floor and saw my bathing suit. When he realized that I had defied him and worn my bathing suit under my clothes, he jerked his belt off of his waist and began hitting my bare behind with it. After he was satisfied that I had learned my lesson, he left me sobbing uncontrollably in the bathroom floor with marks from his belt all over my backside. As I sat on that bathroom floor, I again hoped earnestly for my father to come get me. I had seen pictures of him when I was in Oklahoma, so I squeezed my eyes tightly shut and tried to remember his face. I tried to burn his image into my soul so I wouldn't forget him. I realized he wasn't going to come and get me, but I refused to give up hope.

We lived in two different houses in New Mexico. One was a small white house in the country outside of town. The other was located in base housing just off the military base my stepfather was stationed at. The little white house was the first house we lived in, and life there wasn't too bad. Our stepfather had shown some of his ugly side by then, but not all of it. The school we went to was in town, and the mornings in New Mexico were cold. Emma and I would be told every morning to go and sit in the car to wait for our stepfather. He would start the car and Emma and I would huddle together in the backseat, trying to stay warm. We weren't good enough to stay in the warm house. He didn't want us in there with him and our mother and he let us know it. He would finally come out about the time the car had warmed up, sit down in the driver's seat, and peer back at us disapprovingly. Emma and I would try not to make eye contact with him. He would say things like, "I don't know why you two act like it is so fucking cold! The car is nice and warm. Quit being little babies." At that point, we hadn't even said anything because we knew better than to protest our current situation. Our red little faces and shivering bodies gave away how cold we were, but he didn't care. He was just happy that we were in the car and not in the house while he was getting ready. That way, he didn't have to deal with us.

When we lived in the base house, we attended a different school than the one we went to while living in the little white house. I was developing into a compassionate little girl with a strong love for dogs. Back in South Dakota, we had a puppy named Ranger. He had been banished to the back yard and never trained. As a result, he had knocked me down one day and hurt me. The next day, he was gone and we hadn't had another dog since. I loved every dog I came into contact with, and hoped one day to have a dog of my own. One day, I was playing at recess with friends. A stray dog came up to the fence, begging for attention. My friends and I petted him through the fence and I was instantly in love. I imagined taking him home with me and letting him sleep in my bed. He would surely protect me from my stepfather and be my friend for the rest of my life. As he licked my hand and I tried to think of a name for him and a way to sneak him home, a car drove by. This grabbed the dog's attention and he took off after the car, running as fast as he could to catch up to it. He caught up. The car hit him and he yelped. I can still hear his yelp. He fell to the ground and the car kept going, almost as if the driver didn't realize the dog had been hit. Blood began to flood from his mouth and he lay there crying. I couldn't get through the fence to him and watched him die that day. I was inconsolable for the rest of the day at school. I cried until I got home, when I tried to compose myself so I would not be noticed. My mother noticed that something was wrong and asked me if I was okay. I broke down sobbing and told her about the poor dog and how he had died right in front of me. She sent me to my room to lay down and rest. Every time I closed my eyes, I saw that little dog and heard his yelp. When my stepfather got home, my mother sent him to talk to me. He came into my room acting like he was going to comfort me and sat on the end of my bed. He asked me what was wrong and I began crying again as I told him about the little dog being hit by the car and dying. I will never forget what he said next. He told me that the dog wasn't my dog and since he wasn't my dog, there was no reason to be upset. That day, he tried to take one thing away from me that was a huge part of me. My compassion for animals. He left me in my room, and I continued to cry for that little dog. No one came to comfort me. No one told me they were sorry that I had seen a sweet little dog lose his life. I laid in my room and tried to imagine what my father would say. I imagined he would hug me and be sad about the little dog, just like I was. I missed my father so much, and just kept hoping he would come to get me.

I was old enough in New Mexico for my baby teeth to start coming out. The first time I got a loose tooth, I was incredibly excited. It meant that I was growing up and that the tooth fairy was going to come see me. I proudly showed my mother my loose tooth and she was excited too. She told my stepfather when he got home. He wasn't quite as impressed. After a quick examination of my loose tooth, he determined that I was going to take up his valuable time. It was his belief that a loose tooth needed to be pulled. With a pair of pliers. Every night for a week, he worked on that loose tooth. He grasped it with a pair of pliers, moving it back and forth while I heard what sounded like bones crunching inside of my mouth. I had no idea that this wasn't normal; I thought all parents pulled their kids' teeth with pliers. I would sit through the humiliation each night as he crouched above me, pliers in hand, breathing right in my face, working on getting the tooth out. Each night he would get more frustrated. I was cutting into his precious television time. The more frustrated he got, the less gentle he got. I would sit there, fighting back tears and trying not to show my fear, as he yanked that loose tooth every way possible. I would taste the blood in my mouth and hear the bone crunching and pray that this would be the night the tooth would break loose. Finally after a little over a week, it did. He held the tooth up for me to see as he shoved his disgusting used handkerchief into the gaping hole in my mouth to stop the blood from flowing. The tooth was finally out, but now I had a mouth full of his stinking, dried up snot-covered handkerchief. That began his tradition of pulling my teeth, and my lifelong fear of anyone touching my teeth.

We lived in New Mexico until I was about halfway through the third grade. My best friend was a little girl down the street named Lori. If Lori and I played together, it could only be outside. Emma and I were never allowed to go into anyone's house. Our clothes might be dirty, our hair might be a mess, or we might actually have fun. Our stepfather didn't want us going into anyone's house and he let us know it was because he didn't want us to embarrass him. Lori and I played happily outside and most of the time, Emma joined in. Emma and I both wore glasses and one day, we were down the street playing with Lori and some other kids Lori knew. Our street ended in a cul-de-sac on each end; we lived on one cul-de-sac and the other kids lived on another. Emma's glasses were accidentally broken by another kid. I don't remember if we were playing tag or Red Rover or something like that. Emma went home in a panic because her glasses were broken and she was going to be in trouble. I followed behind her. Our stepfather was home, and by the time I got home, he had already spanked Emma and sent her to her room. A spanking in our home was being hit with a belt on our bare bottoms, and there were usually marks left on us. Spankings were always followed up with being banished to our rooms. As I walked into the house, my stepfather confronted me about Emma's glasses. He wanted to know which "court" the kids lived on that we were playing with. I was in the third grade at the time, and I knew that we lived on Maine Court. So, I told him that the kids were on Maine Court. He got angry with me and spanked me and sent me to my room, because I allegedly was being a smart-ass. I didn't realize that he wanted to know which cul-de-sac the kids lived on.

Emma and I both broke our arms when we were little. I broke mine while we lived in New Mexico. I don't remember how Emma broke hers, but I remember her being hysterical because she thought she was going to be in trouble. Instead of being able to be a kid and just worry about the horrendous pain she was in, she had to walk into the hospital, worried about being in trouble. As we walked into the emergency room, Emma kept crying out, "My daddy's gonna kill me, my daddy's gonna kill me." Our mother tried to calm her down, but once Emma became hysterical calming her down was like trying to pick up a greased pig one-handed on the first try. The hospital staff found it quite amusing, but they didn't realize Emma was being sincere. She truly thought our stepfather was going to kill her. Emma had gotten hurt and drawn attention to herself; she had needed something other than the standard food and shelter. When we got home, our stepfather was not happy. However, instead of hitting her he just grounded her. Emma got grounded for getting hurt. It wasn't long after that when I broke my arm. I had an unfortunate run-in with another kid on a bicycle. We met unexpectedly on a sidewalk one day and I fell over the handlebars of his bicycle, landing on my left hand. I broke my arm in three places. There were also several scrapes, bumps, and bruises. When I went inside, I cleaned up my wounds myself. My mother came to check on me but I told her I was fine. I didn't want to call attention to myself. For three days, I continued telling my mother that I was fine. She checked my arm several times. It was a little swollen but when she turned it different ways and it hurt, I just told her it was fine. Finally on the third day, I rolled over on it accidentally. I hadn't been feeling well and went inside to lay down. Half asleep, I rolled over right on top of it. Pain shot through my entire arm and was so horrendous that I immediately began crying. I went to my mother with tears in my eyes and told her I hurt my arm. She took me to the emergency room. At that point, I didn't care if my stepfather killed me or not. I just wanted the pain to stop. X-rays were done and my arm was broken in three places. It was placed in a cast. When we went home, I expected the insults to begin flying and the worst punishment possible to be handed down. My stepfather didn't say a word, except to say that I shouldn't have waited so long to say something. If I had said something the day I got hurt, I would have been in trouble.

Since I waited three days to say something, I was in trouble for that. There just was no winning with him.

Our mother wasn't allowed to live in peace in our home, either. She and our stepfather got into huge arguments. These started in the base house; the honeymoon period had worn off for them by then. Emma and I would be in our rooms at night, and it seemed that the majority of their arguments happened then. They would scream and curse at one another for hours. Fortunately, our house was separated from the next house by the carport. The neighbors never heard, so the military policemen never came. Sometimes, Emma and I would be together in one room when an argument started. We would huddle together and close our eyes tight, hoping it would just stop. Every time, we worried about him hurting our mother. One time, I think he stabbed her with a screwdriver. We were going to have company and they were trying to put a bed together. They were screaming and cursing, he told her he wanted the Phillips head screwdriver, and all of a sudden, our mother started shrieking in pain. She yelled at him, "Oh my God, you stabbed me with it! What is wrong with you?" Emma and I looked at each other, scared out of our minds. What if he really hurt our mother? Should we go out and try to protect her? We stayed in our room because we knew if we came out without permission, he might stab us too. One time, we were huddled together while they were arguing. There was a bed frame sitting against the wall. Our stepfather pushed our mother, causing her to hit the wall on the other side of the bed frame. The bed frame came crashing down and suddenly, there was dead silence in the house. Emma and I went to the farthest corner of the room and huddled down together. If our stepfather thought we knocked the frame over, we would be in big trouble. The door to the bedroom opened and he peered in. "What the fuck was that?" he yelled at us. Emma pointed to the bed frame and before our stepfather could yell at us some more, our mother stepped up behind him. She realized what happened and stepped between us, pushing him out of the doorway and closing the door. Then she yelled at him for pushing her and causing the bed frame to fall over. The argument lasted for hours while Emma and I stayed in that corner, holding tightly to one another.

When we lived in New Mexico, my stepfather got orders to his next duty station. This time, it was going to be in Holland. I didn't know where Holland was, so my mother showed me pictures of a beautiful land with thousands of flowers and little rivers with boats. There were pictures of hundreds of little bicycles. Holland was somewhere "overseas" and my mother was excited to be moving there. I wasn't. I was going to have to leave Lori and I wasn't going to be able to see my family in Oklahoma anymore. I still hadn't seen my father, and I didn't know how he was going to find me in Holland. The memory of his face was beginning to fade, and I was getting scared that I would forget him. Were we going to have to go on a boat or a plane to get to Holland? There were so many questions and I felt so anxious about moving to Holland, but I couldn't ask. My opinion didn't matter. We were moving to

Holland and that was final. I laid in my bed at night wishing my mother would just let me live with my grandparents or my Aunt Teresa. Maybe if I was really, really good, she would let me live with my father. My stepfather didn't want me there, so I didn't understand why I couldn't just be somewhere that I was wanted. I kept hoping that the whole Holland thing would be a big joke and that we would stay in New Mexico where I could at least see my family sometimes. It wasn't a joke. It was a reality. The day that we left New Mexico, we were told to go tell our friends "goodbye." I went to Lori's house and knocked on the door, but she wasn't home. I went back home to help finish loading our belongings. We left about an hour later. As we drove away, I saw Lori playing in a friend's yard. She was doing cartwheels and she never saw me. I asked if we could please stop so I could tell her goodbye. We didn't stop. I spent the next half hour being yelled at. Not because I did anything wrong, but because I dared to speak up and because I wanted something. I rode in silence and stared at the window, watching New Mexico and Lori disappear on the horizon. It would be over a decade before I returned to the area. I never saw Lori again.

Chapter 3

Europe

Before we moved to Europe, we went to Oklahoma for one last time. Our stepfather had some sort of training to attend, so we were in Oklahoma with our mother. One night, I woke up extremely ill. I was weak and nauseated. We were in our grandparents' apartment in Oklahoma City with our grandparents and our mother. I knew better than to try to wake anyone up. Somehow, I made it to the bathroom just in time to throw up. To my horror as I threw up, I began to experience uncontrollable diarrhea. This went on for a few minutes and then I had a brief moment of relief. In that moment, I desperately tried to clean up the bathroom. I just knew that if the bathroom was a mess, I would be in trouble.

Mere seconds after I had the bathroom clean, the illness struck again. This time I was able to sit on the toilet and hold a trash can. I was shaking from head to toe, and was light-headed. To my horror, my grandmother woke up. She called out to me and asked if I was okay. I told her that I was and she asked if I needed her help. I told her that I didn't. She went back to bed. I was up the entire night, sick as could be. My grandmother woke up two more times and offered her help and I wouldn't take it. I didn't want to be in trouble the next day for disturbing her. The next morning, my grandmother found me curled into a tiny little ball in the bathroom floor. I had been sick all night and was severely dehydrated. As soon as she realized how sick I really was, she woke my mother up. I was taken to the emergency room and diagnosed with the stomach flu. For two more weeks, I was sick. Those were the last two weeks that we were in Oklahoma, and I spent them laying on a pallet in the dining room floor. My mother considered delaying our departure for Europe because I was so sick, but my stepfather wouldn't have it. When it was time for him to go, it was time for us to go. I was loaded up into our old station wagon and took the long drive to the airport in Dallas to begin our journey to Europe.

When we arrived in Holland, things got really bad. We were literally overseas. There was an ocean between us and our family. We were completely at the mercy of our stepfather. Our mother was excited to live in Europe but Emma and I were not. We realized that there would be no visits from our grandparents that would make our stepfather be on his "best" behavior. There would be no trips to Oklahoma without him that would give us a little break from the reality of our daily lives with him. In Holland, there was no escape from him.

Our school in Holland was an international school. We attended with students of several different nationalities to include British, Dutch, German, and Turkish. From the very first day of school, we attended German classes. As a third-grader, I didn't understand that we were stationed at a NATO base overseas at the end of the Cold War. There was significant terrorist activity, and American students had to learn German because we couldn't speak English in public. It was not safe for us. Emma and I learned German quickly, and tried to settle in to our new home. Every night, I would lay in my bed and think about how much ocean there was between me and my father. I worried about how he would find me if he ever tried to look for me. I knew in my heart that it would be years before I saw him again. Still, I kept hoping for him. In the meantime, I had to learn a new culture, a new language, and figure out how to survive living with my stepfather. He had realized that he had a unique power over us in Holland. There was no one to protect us. We had already been conditioned not to talk about what happened at home, so he was safe from us ever telling anyone. His military career was more important than anything to him and we dared not do anything that threatened that.

Not long after we moved to Holland, Emma and I heard a phrase come from our stepfather that truly summed up how he felt about us. He was angry one day; perhaps because we had left a cup out or a door open. Anything that brought attention to us and our existence set him off. As he stood in front of us screaming and cursing at us for whatever infraction we committed, he said, "You two need to remember one thing! All you are is guests in my house. You will never be anything else. As guests you need to respect me and my house." We were only guests in his house. I pondered that for a moment while he continued to scream and curse, while trying to appear that I was still paying attention to him. We were only guests in his house. That meant that we weren't a part of any family. If we were guests there, we weren't a part of his family. That family included our mother. So, we weren't part of our mother's family. The rest of our family was in the U.S. We weren't part of that family because we wouldn't see them for years. We weren't part of our father's family because we weren't even allowed to talk about missing him much less see him. Emma and I weren't a part of anything. We didn't belong anywhere and we didn't belong with anyone. Except each other. Emma was all I had. I was all Emma had. It would be a long five years living in Europe.

Surprisingly, we did return to Oklahoma with our mother the summer after we moved to Holland. Our stepfather had to work and it was an amazing vacation away from him for a couple of months. We stayed with our maternal grandparents in Oklahoma, and our paternal grandparents lived about a mile away. Emma and I still knew not to say anything about the reality of our lives in Holland, even with an ocean between us and our stepfather. At some point, we would have to return to Holland and none of our family would be there to protect us. We remained silent about all of the bad stuff that happened at home, and just tried to enjoy the time we had with family. One morning, about a week after we arrived, I went outside to play while my mother, grandfather, and Emma slept. My grandparents had two dogs by then. One was named Skipper and the other was named Fu. Our stepfather was scared of Fu because Fu would try to protect us if our stepfather tried to act mean toward us around him. On this particular morning, Fu went outside with me. My grandfather liked to gather junk, and in the backyard sat an old combine blade. The individual blades were wood and perfect for playing a game of "tight rope." I climbed up on one blade and began to carefully make my way across, pretending that the ground underneath was hot lava. When I made it to the middle of the blade, the weight from my body snapped the rotted wood in half, and I fell through the blade. I landed on the ground beneath with my right leg still stuck in the jagged edges of the broken blade. My leg was cut deeply from just below my buttock to just above my knee. I couldn't move. Fu went berserk. He whined and cried, dancing around me and then running into the house. A few seconds later he reappeared, ran to me, smelled my leg, whined again, and ran back inside. He repeated this behavior several times as I took inventory of the situation and tried to figure out what to do. My leg was bleeding heavily and hurt like crazy. I realized I needed to make it into the house, clean myself up, and look innocent by the time everyone else woke up. Somehow, I freed my leg from the broken blade. I made my way carefully and quietly into the house, trying to stop the blood from falling to the floor as I walked through the kitchen and into the bathroom. In the bathroom, I looked for something to clean my leg with. I found peroxide and toilet paper. I began to try to clean my leg but it was hard to do because the cut was at the back of my leg. The skin on each side of the deep gash kind of flopped open. I poured peroxide into the gash and felt the searing pain of the peroxide cleaning the wound. I tried hard not to cry. The bleeding wouldn't stop. At the time, I was about nine years old. Instead of risking getting into trouble by waking someone up, I tried to improvise and began to stuff toilet paper into the open wound. The blood soaked quickly into the toilet paper and I soon realized I was getting nowhere. I began to run water in the bathtub, thinking that I would clean my leg that way. By this time, I was getting a little lightheaded. I was determined not to wake anyone because calling attention to myself would only get me into trouble. What I didn't realize during this whole crisis was that Fu kept returning to my grandfather's room, trying to wake him. Fu knew I was hurt and was trying to get help for me. My grandfather finally woke up and followed Fu into the bathroom. What he found was blood all over me and the floor beneath me, and a huge gash in my leg. He looked at the gash and told me that I would need stitches. I tried to tell him I was okay and not to wake my mother. He woke her up anyway and she took me to the emergency room. I had to have stitches to close the wound, and I was afraid the whole time that I would be in trouble. Since my stepfather was still in Holland, I didn't get into trouble.

My mother had a good friend in Holland the first few years we lived there. Her name was Melba, and she was in the Air Force. She was a single mother and had one daughter. She also had a cat that I adored. We would go over to Melba's house to visit sometimes, and my stepfather would always be on his best behavior. I think he was somewhat intimidated by Melba because she was a single woman in the military raising a child on her own. She didn't need a man to help her, and my stepfather didn't know how to handle that. Melba and her daughter lived about a mile away from our house, and sometimes they would come to visit us. At the time, Emma and I shared a room that overlooked the front yard of the home. We were close enough to the next street to see traffic coming down the road. There were many evenings that I would sit in the window and watch traffic coming down the road, hoping that one of the cars that turned down our street would be Melba coming to visit. When Melba came over, our stepfather left us alone. I believe Melba suspected that he abused us, and he felt that if he did something inappropriate in front of her, she would defend us. Our mother wasn't in a position to defend us, but Melba was. Eventually, Melba received orders to Norway and moved away. Our silent savior was gone.

We had always been expected to keep our rooms neat, ever since I can remember. When we lived in South Dakota, I remember picking up tiny pieces of trash from the floor in our bedroom because we didn't have a vacuum cleaner. When we moved to Europe, our stepfather's expectations became higher. He performed white glove inspections in our rooms. If there was the tiniest bit of dust on a surface he would destroy our rooms. If he couldn't bounce a quarter on our beds, he would destroy our rooms. If he opened a drawer and one piece of clothing wasn't perfectly folded, he would destroy our rooms. He would take every piece of clothing out of every drawer and throw it to the ground. Each drawer would come completely out of the dresser and follow the clothes to the ground as well. All of our clothes would come out of the closets and be thrown to the ground. Then he would move on to our beds and remove all of the bedding. The bedding would land on top of the clothes and drawers, then off would come the mattresses. As a final gesture, he would take his arm and sweep anything sitting on top of our dressers onto the floor as well. Then we would have to clean it all up, usually while he stood over us screaming and cursing at us. He would tell us we were guests in his house, we were ungrateful, we weren't worth anything, and we would never amount to anything. The white glove inspections could happen at any time. If he walked into our rooms and we were reading a book, he would ask us if our chores were done. No matter what we said, we were in trouble. If we had done our chores and said so, he would inspect our rooms along with the rest of the house. If anything was out of place or undone, he destroyed our rooms. If we told him our chores weren't done, he would destroy our rooms. We weren't allowed to read books. We weren't allowed to sit quietly in our rooms and take time off from the reality outside of our bedroom doors. We weren't allowed to draw attention to ourselves. No matter what we did, the result was our rooms being destroyed and him standing over us screaming and cursing while we tried to clean up his mess.

The longer we lived in Holland, the more abusive our stepfather became. No matter what we did, we were always in the wrong. Emma and I participated in an extra project at school where we sang in the musical *Annie*. One of the songs was about cleaning a room. As we left the school that day,

Emma and I were so proud of the extra effort we had put into the project. Our mother was proud as well, and when she said something about how great we did, our stepfather quickly retorted that we were worthless because we could sing about cleaning a room but we couldn't actually do it. Emma and I bowed our heads and remained silent for the ride home. Nothing we did was ever going to be good enough for him. He lectured us the rest of the way home and continued to do so for about an hour after we got home. The longer we lived there, the longer his lectures became. If Emma and I did something wrong, we would be called to the living room. We would have to stand at attention (literally) while he screamed and cursed at us about whatever the infraction was. He would continue to say the same thing over and over again, getting angrier by the minute. As he would sit there screaming, his face would turn red. Blood vessels in his forehead would pop out. I would try to fade away into my own head and drown him out with my own thoughts. As he sat there and screamed at us about how worthless and disgusting we were, and how he didn't want us there, I would watch the clock on the VCR behind him. On average, his rants lasted for about three hours. I learned at the early age of about nine years old to stand at attention for up to three hours without moving a muscle. If he got really angry, the lecture would end with us being hit multiple times on our bare bottoms with his belt. Looking back, I think he got some kind of disgusting sexual pleasure out of hitting us like that. He liked to have control.

When I started the 6th grade, an angel walked into my life. Her name was Meredith and she was in my class. She was funny and sweet and we instantly became friends. While I was awkward, always in need of a haircut, wore glasses, was too skinny, and quite ugly, Meredith was the opposite. She was popular and pretty. Meredith always had nice clothes to wear and always looked pretty. She had a heart of gold, and she took me under her wing. Emma and Meredith quickly became friends as well, and we started spending time at Meredith's house every chance we got. The first time I stayed at

Meredith's house, I realized Meredith's family was different from mine. As we rode home on the bus, Meredith told me about her stepmother. Her stepmother stayed home like my mother did, but she actually had some power in the household. Meredith talked about how she asked her stepmother that morning if we could go to McDonald's that night. McDonald's in Holland was expensive and a huge treat. Meredith told me that her stepmother said she would think about it, and Meredith knew that if we got to her house and her stepmother hadn't started supper, we were going to McDonald's. That was Meredith's stepmother's way of telling Meredith's father that she wasn't cooking that night. It took a minute for that to sink in. Meredith's stepmother *told* Meredith's father what she was or wasn't doing. She didn't ask for permission. My own mother had to ask for permission for everything. This even included using the clothes dryer during the day. When we got to Meredith's house, her stepmother greeted us and asked about Meredith's day. We sat in their sunny, pretty kitchen and I was part of the conversation. At home, Emma and I didn't speak much. We weren't allowed to speak unless we were spoken to, and we weren't allowed to actively participate in conversations. We were only allowed to answer questions asked of us. Meredith and I went up to her room. It was neat and pretty, and she had a lot of belongings. She even had a stereo. Emma and I had a stereo at one point but it had been taken away from us and given to our stepsister, without our blessing. Our stereo had been sent to us by our father, so we weren't allowed to keep it. When Meredith's father got home, he came to her room. He knocked on the door and asked permission to come in. Then he hugged Meredith and asked her how her day was. He introduced himself to me and then he told Meredith he loved her and left the room. *He told Meredith he loved her.* Up until that day, I truly believed that fathers didn't want their children, and that all children were burdens to their fathers. Meredith's father *loved* her and he *wanted* her there. That was a completely new concept to me, but it gave me hope that one day, someone would love me.

During our stay in Europe, our step-siblings came to visit a couple of times. The first time, our stereo was taken from us and given to our stepsister. We tried not to hold it against her because it wasn't her decision. Naturally, there was sibling rivalry and bickering between us. For the most part we got along pretty well. At one point our step-siblings planned to live with us for the school year instead of returning to their mother in the U.S. We were all excited. We did our school shopping together, attended orientation at the school, and got all of our supplies. The night before school was supposed to start, our mother woke us up after we went to sleep. A family meeting was called. Everyone went to the living room and sat down. One of our step-siblings had called their mother and they were going back to the U.S. instead of going to school with us. Emma and I didn't know why. We went back to bed and the next morning, they walked down to the bus stop with us. When we were away from the house, out of earshot of our parents, they told us the truth. They had realized how our stepfather treated us and didn't want to live under his roof. They didn't want to become victims like we were. The last time I saw them, they told us that we should go live with our dad. We would be much happier. We got on the bus and rode to school that day, weighing everything they had said. Emma and I agreed that we could not go to live with our dad. It would break our mother's heart and leave her vulnerable to our stepfather. If we weren't there, he would take all of his frustrations out on her. We loved her, and we had to protect her. There was no choice but for us to stay with her.

Christmas time was always special in Holland and the surrounding countries. Our classes would go on field trips to local Christmas markets and we would get a feel of the culture around us. These markets were merry and pretty. Little handmade wooden ornaments adorned shelves in tiny little vendor stands and candy was everywhere one turned. Little gingerbread men and *lebkuchen* was abundant, and we quickly learned how amazing each was. There were even vendors roasting chestnuts at the entrances. For me, it was an escape from the reality of home. I could walk into a Christmas market and be transformed to another world. It was a world where children wandered happily around, and just enjoyed being kids. I didn't have that at home. Emma loved the Christmas markets too, and when we did go to them with our mother and stepfather, we were allowed to wander around by ourselves. It was a rare treat for us. We didn't understand why, but when we moved to Holland, our stepfather implemented a new rule. Emma and I were not allowed to walk next to him and our mother. Anywhere we went, we had to walk behind them. We were also not allowed to talk. When we ate supper out somewhere, we already weren't allowed to speak during the meal. Now, we weren't allowed to talk when we walked somewhere. The rule applied even in the event of speaking to one another. Emma and I just followed behind them, completely silent anywhere we went. The first year that we celebrated Christmas in Holland, there was extra money in the house for the first time ever. Our mother purchased gifts for our family back in the U.S. and mailed them well in advance of the holiday. There were some small gifts hanging from the two lights in the living room. When Emma and I were alone one day, we peeked into the gifts. One was for Emma and the other was for me. Later, I let it slip that we had peeked. We didn't even see what was inside; we only saw that one was for Emma and one was for me. You would have thought we murdered babies and disemboweled them on the town square. First, we were subjected to one of our stepfather's screaming, cursing, you're-worthless-and-I-wish-you-had-never-been-born rants for over an hour. Then we were grounded (it wasn't like we went anywhere anyway, or were even allowed in the living room to watch television), then we were told that Christmas for us was cancelled. No gifts were placed under the tree for us, and we went for about three weeks thinking that we had ruined Christmas for ourselves and them. On Christmas morning, there were several gifts under the tree. We weren't allowed to look at them, and we certainly weren't allowed to open any of them. We just went through the day, thinking Christmas had been cancelled in our house. Late in the day, they decided to let us open the gifts. We had received several things from our family back in the U.S. After we opened everything, it was immediately taken away from us. Little girls that sinned the ultimate sin of peeking at gifts weren't allowed to have the gifts that we received. We were in Holland, thousands of miles away from our family. We hadn't seen our father in forever. There was no way to pick up a phone and call someone. We couldn't communicate with anyone except each other. We spent the day in our rooms, quietly staring at the ceiling. Since we were grounded, we weren't allowed to read books or do anything fun. That Christmas, I really hoped my father would come for me. I wished he would call and ask for me. If he would just call, I could tell him I was sorry for whatever I did that made him go away. I could ask him to come get me, and I could tell him that we weren't wanted at home. He never called. The doorbell never rang and he never came to get me.

Our stepfather became creative about his punishments as time went on. I think he got tired of just hitting us.

Screaming and cursing at us, telling us how worthless we were no longer gave him the kicks that he'd experienced in the past. He found new and emotionally harmful ways to hurt us. If he could hurt our hearts and make us feel unloved, that was much better for him than just physically hurting us. Plus, if someone at school or a friend saw marks on us, his military career would suffer. At some point, he felt that we weren't doing enough around the house. Emma and I cleaned up after ourselves. We did all of the laundry to include the linens every week, beginning at ages 9 and 10. Laundry had to be started after midnight because of the electric rates in Holland. Emma and I were responsible for that; we stayed up overnight to do laundry while they slept. We also did all of the dusting, cleaned all of the floors, did the dishes, cleaned the bathrooms, and did the majority of the cooking. They would leave on the weekends to run errands or just spend time together, and Emma and I would be expected to clean everything. One day, we did something wrong and our stepfather decided that we weren't pulling our weight. His solution was to go "on strike." This meant that he stopped doing absolutely anything around the house. In the past, he would cook on special occasions. That stopped. Suddenly, Emma and I were not allowed to cook. We were expected to feed ourselves, but were not allowed to cook to do so. He would cook for himself, or our mother would cook for herself and him. Emma and I were required to eat things that didn't require cooking. He didn't tell us how long he was going to be "on strike," either. It would commence for whatever amount of time he felt was best. Emma and I would eat things like bread and jelly, or cold sandwiches, or open cans of soup and eat them cold. We didn't go hungry but we did get the message, yet again, that we were worthless and not good enough to be cooked for. This lasted for at least a month. After he came off "strike" he made a huge deal about having to cook for us in the future. We were suddenly allowed to cook again. I don't think it was because he felt we did anything right, but instead, he just got tired of not having his little slaves to cook every meal for him. We were only allowed to cook when it benefited him.

They would leave often, making Emma and I stay home alone. We were expected to do chores while they were gone. If we relaxed in our rooms reading a book, we would be in trouble when we got home. We weren't good enough to watch television in their living room when they were home, so we certainly weren't allowed to enjoy it while they were gone either. Sometimes, we were told not to even leave our rooms while they were gone. It wouldn't be a punishment; we just simply weren't allowed out of our rooms. At times, Emma and I would sneak out of our rooms anyway. Sometimes it was just to sit in the hall together and actually share space with another human. At other times, it would be to sneak downstairs and watch television while a program was being recorded. The television would be set to record something and when the recording started, the television would come on. We could stand on the opposite side of the *shrunk* that separated the living room and dining room and listen to the program together. This helped us to avoid disturbing anything in the living room accidentally, which would give away the fact that we had been somewhere we weren't supposed to be. Our stepfather was suspicious that we had left our rooms one day, and went into a rant. He screamed and cursed at us and told us that he would make sure we didn't leave our rooms. When he and our mother planned to leave again, he told us to go to our rooms. Then, he taped our doors shut with duct tape. If we opened the doors, he would know. There was no way to leave our rooms and then fix the duct tape before he got home. We were trapped. He also took it one step further when he placed string along the walls and across the floors. If we walked across it and broke the string, he would know that we had been out of our rooms. Our days of listening to the television programs were over. That one tiny bit of enjoyment that we got out of our lives was gone.

Emma and I depended on one another daily for survival. Despite that, we still fought like cats and dogs on occasion. Sometimes, our fights went to blows. If we fought, we only did it when we were home alone. The punishment for fighting far outweighed the satisfaction of the fighting itself. We usually fought over silly things, but the underlying cause was that we had to get our frustrations out somehow. I knew that Emma was all I had and that she would not turn her back on me, even if we did fight. She knew the same about me. In a way, being able to fight one another helped us relieve stress that was tearing us down. One day, we were washing dishes together. We were both frustrated and angry because of something our stepfather had done. Forgetting that he was in the house, we started to bicker back and forth. Within seconds, he was in the kitchen. We immediately stopped bickering, but it was too late. The show he had been watching had been interrupted by the reminder of our existences, and he was pissed. He stomped over to us and grabbed us each by the hair on the back of our heads. In unison, he shoved our faces down into the sink below us. It was a double sink and mine was the side with the soapy water. Emma was over the side with the rinse water. The end of my nose was in the hot, soapy water. I realized Emma's nose was probably in the rinse water. For a solid ten minutes, he screamed and cursed at us while holding our faces down in the sinks. During that entire time, our mother sat in the living room and did not intervene. I truly believe she felt powerless to stop him. My back throbbed in agony and I desperately needed to use the bathroom. For that entire time, I listened to how worthless and disgusting I was, and how worthless and disgusting Emma was. I heard about how he didn't want us there, and we were not being good "guests" in his house. He taunted us, asking us why we would interrupt his program but knowing that if we answered, he would shove our faces further down into the water. As he screamed and cursed, our heads bobbed in and out of the water. There were a few times that my lungs were screaming for air as I held my breath waiting to be let up again. He was too strong for us and our mother wasn't intervening. We just had to hope and pray that he didn't drown us. I worried for Emma because I couldn't see her. Was she okay? She was silent just like me. Was she able to breathe? Was he going to drown her? I don't know how I didn't panic and start fighting back. Maybe it was self-preservation because I knew if I fought back in any way whatsoever, I would pay dearly. This was the first time I had feared for my life. All because we interrupted his television program.

Living in Holland had its perks. We did get to travel throughout Europe extensively and visited Germany, Italy, Belgium, and France. There were military bases scattered throughout Europe and we went to a few of them rather often. Whenever we traveled, the rules in the car were specific. We still were not to speak unless spoken to. Under no circumstances were we to call any attention to ourselves or any needs we might have. During the entire drive, we were not allowed to read any books. Further, we were not allowed to sleep. If we had to use the bathroom, we had to hold it until he decided to stop. If we were sick, we were out of luck. Our one option when traveling was to look out the window and "enjoy the scenery." Our mother and stepfather smoked ceaselessly. It did not matter if the windows were up or down; they smoked one cigarette after another. I was asthmatic, though I didn't know it at the time. The cigarette smoke exacerbated my asthma, and I spent entire trips trying desperately to breathe without wheezing. If I wheezed, it would call attention to me. Emma had bladder problems and needed to use the bathroom often. When we traveled, she was out of luck. She couldn't even go to sleep to escape the feeling of needing to use the bathroom. She had to sit there, in silence, and suffer. I had to do the same. On one trip in particular, I got car sick. Between riding in the car, breathing in the constant cigarette smoke, and trying not to wheeze, I was severely nauseated. I had to throw up. I managed to tell my mother. She looked over at her husband and asked him to pull over. He refused. We had stopped to eat previously, and I had an almost empty cup in my lap. Since he couldn't be bothered to pull over, I had to throw up in the cup. Then I had to hold that cup, full of vomit, until we stopped. If he didn't want to stop somewhere, we weren't stopping. It didn't matter the circumstances.

There were some good times with our mother and stepfather. Many times, we would go to amusement parks in

Europe. If our stepfather was in a good mood, the day would go well and we would have fun. On days that he was in a bad mood, we would get about halfway to our destination and he would either pick a fight with our mother, remember some horrible crime Emma and I had committed in the past and already been punished for, or suddenly become ill and have to return home immediately. If Emma and I had done something a year, two years, or even ten years before and he remembered it, we were punished all over again. We would spend the entire ride home listening to him rant about whatever it was. If he picked a fight with our mother, they would scream at one another the entire way home while Emma and I sat in silence in the back seat. If he was ill, then we would listen to him groan about how miserable he was the whole time. On the days that we actually made it to the amusement park, we would have a great time. Typically, Emma and I would be allowed to explore the park while our mother and stepfather went their own way. We would return to a designated meeting place at a particular time and go home. He would be in a good mood all the way home and tell us good night as we climbed into bed after a long day of fun. The next day, we would pay. As soon as we woke up, we were in trouble. He would find something from the day before that wasn't clean or he would remember something we had done in the past. As soon as we went downstairs, he would rant and scream at us for whatever it was. Then we would be banished to our rooms. On the rare occasions that we weren't banished, we would be told to clean the house. If that was the case, he would follow us around and criticize everything we did. Dust rags would get yanked out of our hands and we would be slapped across the face with them. Trash cans would get overturned and we would have to clean them up. Dirty ashtrays would be shoved under our noses and we would be asked why they weren't spotless. No matter what we did, it wasn't right. It didn't take us long to learn his pattern. If he did something nice for us, we would always pay the next day.

The last Christmas that our mother was in Europe with us was the worst. The rule had been established long before that we were to eat everything on our plates, no matter what. This rule was especially difficult for me because I suffered from frequent migraines. If I came home from school with a migraine, I still had to eat my supper before I could go to bed. The only reprieve I got was not having to help with dishes after supper. I would sit at the table, by myself, for about an hour, trying to choke down the food in front of me. Migraine symptoms include nausea and sensitivity to light. I just wanted to lay down in a cool, dark room and go to sleep. Until everything was gone from my plate, I couldn't. On this particular Christmas, Emma wasn't feeling well. We always had one meal on Christmas, usually at about 6 p.m. During the day, we were allowed to snack on a "relish tray" that consisted of chopped vegetables and dips. If we filled up during the day, we still had to eat everything on our plates at supper. It didn't matter that it was Christmas. The rules still applied. Emma and I had snacked during the day and she was full. Our mother had made a rum cake for dessert. For over an hour, Emma and I tried to choke down our meals. After about half an hour, our stepfather became angry because we weren't done eating. He began to make snide remarks from the living room about how ungrateful we were and how we better eat quick or we would be sorry. The more time passed, the sicker Emma felt. She was able to finish her meal, but I would have sworn her face turned green. Instead of just letting her leave the table, our stepfather insisted (from his throne in the living room) that she eat a piece of the rum cake. This particular rum cake was one that should have been set afire (literally) to burn off the excess rum before eating. He did not do that. He plopped a heaping piece of rum cake down on our plates and told us to hurry up. Emma looked like she was going to pass out. She ate a few bites and stopped. Then she was yelled at from the living room to hurry up. She tried. Truthfully, she tried. Then she stood up. There was still some cake on her plate. I watched her as she staggered a little bit, with the strangest look on her face. Then she vomited in the dining room. Instead of helping her, or even feeling bad for treating her badly while she was sick, our stepfather began screaming and cursing at her for throwing up in the dining room. He couldn't believe that she would have the nerve to waste food that he worked hard for and paid good money to put on the table. We both went to bed that night, sad and upset. Emma was sick and I was worried about her. Still, I kept hoping that my father would come. I laid in bed that night, willing the phone to ring. More than anything, I wanted him to be on the other end of the line saying that he was coming to get me. I knew if he came to get me, he would take Emma too. Anywhere Emma went, I went. Anywhere I went, Emma went. We were a package deal and wanted him more than anything in the world. He didn't come. The phone didn't ring. We woke up in Hell the next day, again.

There was a little base my mother and stepfather liked to go to sometimes. It was a few hours from our house, and we stayed in the military billeting when we went. They liked having a little overnight getaway sometimes, and for some reason felt it was necessary to take Emma and I with them. We stayed in the same location each time we went. Our suite was comprised of a living area with bunk beds, a small kitchenette, then a door that led to a small bathroom and bedroom. Whenever we stayed there, Emma and I would sleep on the bunk beds in the living area. The door to the bathroom and bedroom remained closed after everyone went to bed, and we were not allowed to open it. On our first trip there, I woke up in the middle of the night. I had to use the bathroom. As I laid there, I willed myself to go back to sleep so I wouldn't realize I needed to urinate. No matter what, I couldn't fall back asleep. I couldn't get up and use the bathroom because that would wake them up and I would be in trouble. At the time, I was about ten years old. Finally, I couldn't stand it anymore. I got up and went to the farthest corner of the room. I squatted there and urinated on the carpet. Then I crawled back into bed, ashamed and mortified. How did that just happen? Had I been reduced to an animal urinating anywhere that was available? I never told anyone, not even Emma. I hoped that the spot was dry by morning. When I woke up the next day, I couldn't even bring myself to look in that corner. Fortunately, my secret was not discovered. The next time we went, the same thing occurred. This time, I had even been sure to use the bathroom before the door was closed for the night. Again, I laid in that bed willing myself to go to sleep. Again, the urge to urinate wouldn't calm down. Again, I squatted like an animal in that very same corner and urinated. Squatting there like an animal was safer than opening that door and risking waking them up. Again, I crawled back into bed full of shame and mortified with myself. My secret was not discovered the next morning, but I still held it in my heart for years to come. I had been reduced to not even being able to meet basic needs. I was truly nothing.

The last year that we were in Europe, our mother earned her GED. She wanted to further her education and enrolled in a college in Pasadena, Texas. At the time, Emma had just gotten her braces off. I was supposed to get braces before our mother left for college. Originally, Emma and I were supposed to go to college with her, leaving our stepfather in Europe. We had to go to the orthodontist, which was over an hour away from our home. On one visit, the orthodontist asked how we were doing. One of us mentioned our mother going to college in the U.S. and us going along. Little did we know, if my braces were put on in Europe, the military wanted me to stay in Europe as long as my stepfather was there. Once our stepfather found out that the trip back to the U.S. had been mentioned, he blew up. We were marched out of the orthodontist's office, and made to stand by benches outside. He sat on one bench and began one of his rants. Since we were in public, he spoke softly and made sure no one could hear him cursing at us. Ultimately, since one of us spoke up about something that was occurring at home (which was prohibited) he decided that both of us were just going to have to stay in Europe with him. Our mother would be allowed to go to Pasadena for school, but we would not. The one person that kept him somewhat calm, and kept him from killing us, was going to be leaving. We were going to be stuck thousands of miles away from our family, even our mother, and he was going to have complete control of us.

Shortly before her first college semester started, our mother left us. I was grounded at the time because my stepfather found Monopoly money under my pillow one day. I had just been playing "bank" and wasn't doing anything wrong. He got it in his head that I had been cheating during a Monopoly game. Once he decided Emma or I had done something, there was no way to redeem ourselves. It didn't matter if we were innocent or not. As a result, I had missed out on spending time with our mother before she left. This was heavy on my heart as we traveled to the airport with her and waved goodbye while she walked to the gate for her departure. As we got into the car to head home, an overpowering sense of doom came over me. Now, it was just me, him, and Emma. What was going to happen to us? Were we going to be able to satisfy him enough that we would not be beaten or ridiculed every day we were alone with him? Was he going to be even meaner since our mother was gone? Why couldn't we just go stay with our father for the year? It seemed like the longest ride home ever. I didn't know what was going to happen when the door to the house closed behind us, and we weren't in the relative safety of the public. The same things must be running through Emma's mind. Since our mother wasn't in the car and we weren't allowed to speak, the entire car ride was silent. I had never felt so utterly alone in my entire life.

Not long after our mother left, our lease was up at our house. We had to move to a different house, which was located in another town close by. The house we had been living in was old and beautiful. It had a huge garden in the back that I had tended for the last four years. It was on a quiet little street, and I had grown quite fond of the place. The movers came and we went to our new destination. Our new house was a little more modern and didn't have a garden in the back. There was nowhere for me to escape. The house did have three floors. The attic was an additional bedroom. Emma and I chose to use that as our bedroom. Our stepfather was on the floor below us. I imagined Emma and I were like the children in *Flowers in the Attic*. The attic was our escape and if we were very, very quiet, no one would know we were there. We could truly keep our existence a secret and manage to stay off our stepfather's radar. Unfortunately, my imagination and the reality of the situation didn't match up. What followed was, by far, the worst year of our lives.

Without our mother there, our stepfather had no need to control his anger with us. He made it obvious from the first moment we were home without our mother, that he didn't want us there. "If you two would just act right, I could spoil you like I do your mother. But you're too stupid to do that, so it's never going to happen," he would say to us. He loved to tell us how stupid we were, and how he didn't want to have to take care of us. Since our mother was gone, he could tell us repeatedly how we were worthless, and how we would never amount to anything. "You two aren't good for anything but reproducing and being housewives. Look at Emma, she already has breeder hips. She's going to be able to pop out babies easy," was something else he would tell us. He loved to put us down. The worse he made us feel about ourselves, the better he felt. It wasn't until I was grown that I realized he said those things out of insecurity about himself. If he could lift himself up by tearing us down, he could feel better about his own failures. I was grown and had children of my own before I realized he was the true failure in that house. He couldn't even love a ready-made family.

Money got tight while we were in Europe for that last year. He was having to support two households; ours in Europe and our mother's in Pasadena. The tighter money got, the angrier he got. Naturally, his anger was taken out on us. He began to drink heavily and the more he drank, the more easily the insults rolled off his tongue. Emma and I would stay in our attic hideaway as much as we could, but if we didn't hear him yelling for us, there would be Hell to pay. One day, we were eating at the table. He had a friend over and they were watching a game on the television. He came into the living room and began to joke around with us. It didn't take even half a second to realize that he was drunk out of his mind. Emma and I tried to just not make eye contact with him and hoped he would leave. He didn't. His friend continued to watch the game and our stepfather's attempts to joke with us turned into anger. Emma was finished with her meal and she got up to leave the table. She was told to sit down. Emma didn't comply immediately and instead, turned to leave the room. Our stepfather followed her, hurling insults at her. Emma just wanted to get safely to our bedroom. As she reached for the door to the stairs, our stepfather staggered in front of her. Emma changed course and walked toward the living room, thinking that the friend would intervene. The friend continued to watch the game, acting as if he didn't hear anything that was going on less than 20 feet away. By this time, our stepfather was enraged. He pushed Emma to the ground and laid on top of her. With his face less than an inch from hers, and his fat, disgusting body covering her 95 pound frame, he began one of his rants. I could smell the alcohol from where I was seated, about 10 feet away. His rant continued for a good hour, with

Emma unable to move and me frozen in my spot. Finally, he decided that he was done and rolled off of her. Emma and I both tore for the door to the stairs. We didn't come out of our rooms for the rest of the night. The following morning, he acted as if everything was okay. I'm sure that he was so drunk he didn't remember what he did that night. It never left my mind that he would, at some point, hurt us in a sexual way. Emma and I both realized that was a possibility and it scared the life out of us. However, his military career was incredibly important to him. Leaving marks on us and emotionally abusing us probably wouldn't get him kicked out of the military, but sexually abusing us would. His military career was our saving grace.

One unfortunate reality of our mother being gone, as if there weren't enough already, was that he was responsible for all of our dental and medical appointments. My braces had been installed, and I had to have my wisdom teeth out. It is likely that this was done while we were in Europe so it would be covered by the military and not cost him out of pocket. My stepfather never even told me I had an appointment. He showed up at school one day and picked me up. I knew better than to ask where we were going. That would remind him that I was in the car and that he was having to miss work for my worthless, stupid self. I remained silent in the car and didn't realize where we were going until we arrived at the dentist's office. Once inside, I couldn't ask the dentist while my stepfather was in the room. That would break the "don't speak unless you're spoken to" rule. Finally, my stepfather left the room and I asked the dentist as quietly as I could (so my stepfather wouldn't overhear) what he was going to do that day. He explained he had to pull a few of my teeth. I didn't ask anything after that. The appointment itself wasn't too bad, but the dentist took things slowly and tried to minimize my pain and comfort me in my anxiety. He ensured that my mouth was nicely numbed ad then cut my wisdom teeth out. A few stitches later and I was good to go. We left the dentist's office and returned home. Immediately, I went up to my room. I had homework to do and knew better than to get behind. If we made a C or below on anything, we were grounded until the next report card. Once I was in my room, the numbness in my mouth began to wear off. My stepfather was watching television downstairs. I knew better than to interrupt him. I stayed in that room, alone and in pain. He never checked on me. An offer of pain medication, an ice pack, or something soft to eat was never made. Later that evening, I was expected to go downstairs and cook with Emma. I had to eat everything on my plate and help with the dishes afterward. By the time I laid down in my bed that night, I was exhausted. The pain in my mouth was the most intense, horrible pain I had felt in my entire life.

One of the many rules in our house was related to food. Emma and I were allowed to take lunches to school, but were limited to what we could take. When our mother was gone, we were allowed to take a sandwich and one snack. He liked Pringles, and we were not allowed to touch those. The Pringles container was monitored closely and if he had the slightest suspicion that we had eaten even one of them, he would rant incessantly. One of my favorite things was Fruit Roll-Ups. When I ate one, I wanted another one. That could easily turn into three. I lacked self-control when it came to them. The Fruit Roll-Ups disappeared at a rapid pace because of my addiction, and he noticed quickly. He never said anything, and instead came up with a creative way to alleviate my problem. One morning, he left for work. We watched him disappear down the road and around the corner. I went to the kitchen and began making my lunch for the day. After I got my lunch packed, I took a yummy little Fruit Roll-Up, exceeding my daily quota, and sat down in the living room with it. I was breaking two rules: one too many snacks and sitting in the living room. As I savored the taste of that sweet strawberry heaven, I glanced over to my left and out the window. Standing in front of the house on the sidewalk and peering in was my stepfather. He had caught me red-handed. I had the snack in my mouth and was sitting on the sofa, and he saw me clearly. There was nowhere to go. I couldn't hide. He came into the house, enraged. Off came his belt and down went my pants. It was the first time I had been hit on my bare bottom in a long time, and I was completely powerless. I was fourteen years old at the time and well into puberty. The entire experience was humiliating. I fought to hold back tears and had no way to cover my naked rear end. When he stopped hitting me, he started screaming and cursing at me. My entire bottom screamed in pain and I was afraid to move much less pull up my pants. Fortunately, he couldn't scream and curse for as long as he normally would because he would be late for work. He realized how late it already was and stomped out of the house, slamming the door. I pulled up my pants and looked down at the wrapper on the ground. That one snack wasn't worth the beating and humiliation I had just endured. For the first time in my life, I tried to think of a way to retaliate. He loved his Pringles. He still counted them and made sure we didn't eat any. We weren't good enough to eat his Pringles. I went into the kitchen and took down his container of Pringles. I removed the first four or five and set them to the side. Then I licked the next few Pringles and placed the dry ones on top. I continued this with the other two containers of Pringles. A few days later, when he had eaten some out of each container, I repeated my lick-and-return method. I continued this for the remainder of our stay in Europe.

During the time we remained in Europe with our stepfather, he claimed to be working two jobs. There were many nights that he would "work" overnight and we would go to a friend's house to stay. Emma and I would go together, and it was almost always on school nights. The friend was Tracy Smythe and she had two daughters just a little younger than Emma and I. Her husband worked with our stepfather. Tracy was not what we were used to. She worked part-time at the commissary and made her own money. Her husband didn't have much say in the running of their home or how their children were raised. One day, he got angry because their eldest pulled the sheets off the waterbed and tore one. Instead of the child getting into trouble, the husband was in hot water for getting on to the child. Tracy ran her home with a love and protectiveness I hadn't seen before. I knew my mother loved us dearly, but she wasn't able to protect us. Tracy's kids were allowed to wander around the neighborhood. They had bicycles and friends all over the place. Tracy had a little Yorkshire Terrier that she adored. When I was at Tracy's house, I could ride a bicycle or take the dog on a walk any time I wanted. If I wanted to watch TV, I could. Tracy would make supper and we would all wash dishes together. Even though Tracy worked outside of the home, she still came home and did things for her family. We could eat all the snacks we wanted at Tracy's house, and the Pringles weren't counted. I looked forward to going to Tracy's house because I could just be a kid for a while. Emma loved going to Tracy's house too. She was a ray of sunshine in our dark, sad lives. It wasn't until years later that I realized Tracy had to know what was going on in our home. She had to have seen bruises on us and the sadness in our eyes. Yet, she did absolutely nothing to protect us. The one woman that protected her own home and family and incredible ferocity did nothing to protect the two young girls that were being abused right under her nose.

While our mother was living in Pasadena, I started my menstrual cycle for the first time. I knew what to expect and what to do because Emma had forewarned me. The pain and cramping that first time was horrible. For two full weeks, my cycle raged. I was going through hormonal ups and downs that I had no idea how to deal with. There was nothing in the house to help with my pain and cramping, and I just suffered through it. I realized at night time that I could sleep in a little ball and that would help somewhat. By this time, I had given up on my father coming to get me or even calling. My mother was thousands of miles away in Pasadena. The incident involving my wisdom teeth was still fresh on my mind. I knew better than to ask for anything to make me feel better. Instead, I just took proper care of the hygiene issues that arose with my cycle and literally limped through the pain for two weeks. Emma knew what was wrong with me and tried to comfort me the best that she could. At some point during that two weeks, I left something out in the bathroom. I don't remember what it was, perhaps a shampoo bottle. My stepfather found it and went into one of his rages. He couldn't believe that we would have the nerve to leave something out in the bathroom that he used too. Emma and I were called to the bathroom where he began his usual screaming and cursing routine. It was painful just to stand there and listen to him, and I began to get lightheaded. I tried to hold myself steady and not make it obvious that something was wrong with me. If I called attention to myself, it would just make things worse. My entire abdomen felt like it was being ripped out. I could feel blood oozing from my body and wanted nothing more than to lay down in my little ball and die. Emma knew I was in horrific pain. She could see the lack of color in my face and realized I was doing everything possible to remain composed and not cry. That's when she did something for me that I will never forget. She interrupted the evil, disgusting man in front of us and told him that she left the bottle out. I started to protest, but she quietly patted my hand. That evil, disgusting man turned to me and told me to leave the room. I pleaded with Emma with my eyes not to take what I knew was coming to her. Something in her eyes told me to leave. I did. I went up to our bedroom and laid on my bed, letting the tears roll down my cheeks and the pain rip through my body. Emma took the beating for me that day, because she knew that I couldn't take it. She realized that something was seriously wrong with me and stood up for me. She did something that is the job of a mother, and she was my sister. Years later and lots of pain later, I found out that I suffered from endometriosis. The condition caused me to miscarry my first baby and required surgical intervention twice. That day in the bathroom, I was experiencing pain similar to childbirth. I just didn't realize it. Something in my face told Emma, though, and she took care of me.

In November 1989, the Berlin Wall came down. The Cold War was coming to an end, and the atmosphere across

Europe changed. In Holland, things had been relatively peaceful with the exception of terrorist activity in the area. That peacefulness began to spread across Europe, and the people around us became much happier than they had been in the past. Many parties took place across Europe and former residents of East Germany began to move into the eastern part of Holland, where we were located. As the Wall came down, many different issues had to be dealt with. One issue was the rehoming of the guard dogs assigned to the Wall. These dogs had been trained to guard the Wall, which was a job they had held their whole lives. They were beautiful German Shepherds that knew nothing other than pacing back and forth in front of tons of cement and barbed wire, ensuring that no one came across the Wall when and where they weren't supposed to. This became a new source of terror our stepfather brought to us. If we didn't behave like the little angels he wanted us to be, he would buy one of those dogs and bring it home. They were guard dogs, not family dogs, he would remind us. If we misbehaved, he would make sure the dog took care of the problem. My entire life, I had loved dogs. I still hadn't forgotten the dog that was hit by the car in New Mexico and my stepfather's reaction to my grief. One of the worst things he could have told me was that he was going to bring a dog home with the express purpose of hurting me. Again, he tried to kill my love for animals. Again, he failed miserably. I held on to my faith that dogs were good and wouldn't hurt me, ever. That's a faith I still hold today.

Emma had an especially difficult time that year. She was a freshman in high school and she had more of a fighting spirit than I did. She knew we weren't being treated right and she talked to a friend at school about it. At one point, Emma went to school with bruises on her arm from where our stepfather had grabbed her one day. Her friend saw the bruises and insisted Emma go to the office with her. As they sat in front of the principal, the friend recounted everything that Emma had told her about our stepfather and everything that was going on at our home. Emma was terrified. The friend mentioned the bruises. The principal turned to Emma and asked if any of this was true. Emma didn't know what to say. She was terrified that if she said something and our stepfather found out, we would both be beaten. If she said something and the principal didn't believe her, we would be in worse shape than we already were. She denied everything the friend said and refused to show the principal her bruises. The principal didn't follow up and we both went home that day. The seed had begun to grow within Emma; she knew that what was happening at home wasn't right. A short time later, our stepfather hurt his foot at work. He had to wear a special boot for a while and was on crutches. Emma and I got into trouble one day as we sat at the table eating our supper. Our stepfather managed to yank us both by the hair and shove us into corners in the living room despite his injury. We stood there for over an hour; I knew how much time had elapsed because he had watched multiple episodes of a television program. The longer we stood there, the madder Emma got. She decided she was going to leave, and she turned around and told our stepfather that. He told her she wasn't going anywhere and she proceeded to walk right out the door. Our stepfather turned to me and told me that if I didn't catch her and convince her to come back, he was going to beat me within an inch of my life. I ran after Emma and caught her about a block down the road. As I caught up to her, I realized that she was so scared, she had urinated on herself. She was hysterical and said she was going to call a friend to come get us. I knew the military police wouldn't believe us, and I knew if I went back to the house without her, I was going to take a beating. There was nowhere for us to go. We had no money, no passports, and no family there. We could make a telephone call but it would take hours for anyone to get to us, if they even bothered to come. We had no choice but to return to the house. When we went back, he beat both of us. I don't know how he managed to stand up long enough to hit us as much as he did, but he left bruises on me that stayed for weeks.

Our stepfather was extremely particular about our hair. Emma and I both had long, thick hair. It took forever to dry and we didn't have a blow dryer. One day, we went to the swimming pool after school. We showered and towel-dried our hair to the best of our ability before our stepfather picked us up. He wanted to go to the track to walk because he had a physical coming up. Our stepfather was a bit on the heavy side and he made the entire household miserable when he had physicals coming. Due to being in the military, he had to stay under a certain weight. He would let himself go for months and then go on crash diets and walk for hours, trying to get the weight off. As we pulled up to the track that day, he was already in a bad mood. We knew not to do anything to set him off when he was in a bad mood, so Emma and I had been completely silent and tried not to make eye contact with him during the ride. He turned to Emma and realized her hair was still damp. He yanked hard on her hair, asking her why she didn't dry it. She told him that she tried. Then he turned to me and yanked on my hair, causing my neck to snap back. When he realized my hair was damp as well, he became enraged. He began screaming at us in the car, cursing at us and telling us how stupid we were. He ended his rant by slapping us each across the face and telling us that we were not to leave the car until our hair was dry. Then he opened his door, got out, and slammed it so hard that the entire car shook. As he walked away, Emma and I looked at one another, shocked. We couldn't believe he pulled our hair and hit us because our hair was damp. We tried our best to dry our hair with our damp towels, but it was useless. By the time he came back to the car, our hair was still damp. As a result, he screamed at us on the entire drive home. When we got home, we had to make his supper for him. Then we had to go to bed without eating. Due to having damp hair, we were screamed at, cursed at, had our hair pulled, were slapped, and went to bed hungry.

For some reason, during that last year in Europe with him, our stepfather decided that we should learn how to iron his uniforms for work. We were definitely old enough to learn how to iron; I was in 8th grade and Emma was a freshman. However, neither of us was ready for the perfection that he expected. He decided he would "train" us on the proper way to iron. Armed with a can of spray starch, an ironing board, and an iron, he set up in one of the spare bedrooms and had Emma and I take turns demonstrating our sudden expertise Emma and I didn't know the first thing about ironing. Instead of teaching us how he wanted it done, he had us demonstrate our skills and then ridiculed us for not knowing what we were doing. We were awarded for our efforts with more of his screaming and cursing. He wanted to know how two girls could be so utterly worthless. Why couldn't we just do what he wanted? Emma and I remained completely silent as he continued his verbal assault for several minutes. As he screamed, cursed, and spit on us, he ironed one of his shirts. "Now pay attention, dumb-asses. This is how I want it done," he yelled at us as he slammed the iron down on the shirt and slid it across the fabric. "Nice and stiff! The creases need to be perfect. If you do it, and I don't like it, you will have to do it again. Don't be stupid and fuck it up like you fuck everything else up," he screamed as he picked the shirt up and shoved it on the hanger. Next came the pants, along with a constant barrage of insults. He finished one uniform and then told us he wanted the rest done by the time he got home. After he walked out of the front door and slammed it behind him, Emma and I looked at each other. We were completely perplexed. He wanted perfection from the first moment. This was the case with everything and something we should have expected by then. We worked together that night on those uniforms, ironing them to the best of our ability. After we were done ironing, we still had homework to do. The grades we made had to be perfect, just like everything else. As I worked on my homework that night, I wondered why he expected perfection out of us. We weren't wanted. He reminded us of that daily. He didn't want us, our mother didn't want us, and our absent father never wanted us to begin with. We were worthless. If we were such sad examples of human beings like he said, how could we also be perfect at the same time?

One evening, Emma and I were in the kitchen doing the dishes after supper. We had a double sink in this house, too. Emma washed while I rinsed and dried. Our stepfather had been drinking a lot since our mother left. This night was no exception. We never heard him walk up behind us and we had broken a major rule; we were talking quietly to one another. Suddenly, we were both grabbed by the hair and he was shoving our faces into the water below. Emma got the worst of it because her water was soapy. Mine was clear. He screamed and cursed at us, letting our heads up for a few seconds here and there so we could catch our breath. Then he would shove our faces down again. I kept my eyes shut tightly and held my breath as long as I could, all the while praying that he wouldn't break our glasses. If they got broken, we would be punished for that too. My back, neck, and legs were screaming in pain from being bent over like that. I knew Emma was feeling the same way. The whole time, I couldn't see her. I don't remember which one of us reached out, but at one point we were squeezing one another's hands. As we did that, I prayed he wouldn't see. If he caught us holding hands and trying to comfort one another, he would beat us for sure. Then, just as suddenly as he started, he let go of our hair and stopped screaming. He walked out of the kitchen without saying a word, leaving Emma and I shaking and staring at one another in silence. We didn't say a word as we wiped our faces dry and finished cleaning the kitchen. After that, I started practicing holding my breath when I was in swimming class. I would start at one end of the pool, swim to the very bottom of the deep end, swim along the bottom, and up the other side. The entire time I would hold my breath. When I mastered this, I knew he would not be able to drown me. It never occurred to me that no child should have to learn to hold their breath for so long so their parent wouldn't be able to drown them.

While our mother was gone, our stepfather found a new way to taunt us. Emma and I were both painfully skinny. I weighed about 98 pounds and Emma weighed about 85 pounds. We were always in need of a haircut and we shared all of our shabby little clothes. Both of us wore glasses with thick lenses because our vision was so poor. Emma had beautiful straight teeth and I had a mouth full of braces. He loved to call us things like "four eyes," "brace face," "thunder thighs," and "potato butt." He always reminded us we would never be good for anything but making babies, saying "you two will never be anything but barefoot, pregnant, and in the kitchen." Emma was by far the prettier of the two of us, and he focused most of his taunts on her. He did his best to make her feel bad about her appearance. "You two have faces not even a mother could love," he would sneer at us. "She's in Texas going to school because she couldn't stand to look at your ugly faces anymore," he said one particular night that he had been drinking. What made matters even worse was that he was an extremely unattractive man. He was always about ten pounds over the weight he should be, he had ugly black hair, an unattractive face, and he wore glasses too. His teeth were yellow and his breath was always horrible. He did not practice good hygiene at all. The insults coming from him were even more hurtful because he was such a disgusting human being both inside and outside. If he found us so ugly, who on this earth would ever find us pretty?

In May of 1990 we were set to return to the United States. At this point, we had been in Europe for five years and this was the longest we had ever stayed in one place. I was torn between returning home to my mother and family, and leaving Meredith and my other friends behind. I would be starting high school in August of 1990, and was scared about starting in yet another new school. In third grade, I attended three different schools. For five years, I had attended one school and only had to be the new girl in class once. Picking up and moving terrified me. What terrified me even more was my family finding out that the previous year had been the worst of my entire life. I didn't want people to know that my stepfather was abusive. If people knew, then that made it real. As long as people didn't know, it was still a secret and somehow not a reality. I didn't have to admit that I was unworthy of someone's love and that I was so disgusting, I had to be beaten and ridiculed on an almost daily basis. The beatings had slowed down, but the ridicule did occur multiple times daily. We still weren't allowed to speak unless we were spoken to first, and I was unsure how I would make new friends. I was socially awkward, as was Emma. We had gotten into trouble at a local restaurant recently because a school friend came to speak to us and we responded. We absolutely were not allowed to speak while we were eating. My brain was so confused about when and if I could speak, that I didn't even know what to say in situations where I actually could speak. By this time, Emma and I had been so browbeaten that we always walked with our heads down and our eyes averted. We felt worthless and ugly, and didn't want to bother anyone. Also, what would my family think if they realized how my stepfather was? Would they agree that we deserved to be treated that way, or would they say it was normal? Was it normal? It wasn't normal in Meredith's house or Tracy's house. My mind was a constant battlefield in itself, weighing the pros and cons of returning to the U.S. Ultimately, I didn't have a choice and late in May 1990, we boarded a plane to return home. I watched Belgium disappear when the plane took off, the buildings and cars becoming smaller and smaller as we climbed higher and higher. We were seated away from our stepfather, so Emma and I were able to relax somewhat on the flight back. I was ready to see my mother but afraid that she would be angry when she found out how horrible Emma and I had been for the last year. For hours, I was a bundle of nerves.

We arrived in Dallas late at night and our mother and maternal grandparents were at the airport waiting for us. After we gathered our luggage, we went to a local Denny's to eat. Our stepfather was on his best behavior because our grandparents were there. They hadn't seen us in four years and were ready to make up for lost time. We were allowed to order a huge ice cream sundae and ate quietly while the adults talked. I was exhausted and ready to lay down. Emma was as well. It was hot and humid in Dallas, even at 2 a.m. The climate in Europe was much better and the trip itself had exhausted us.

My grandmother realized how tired we were, and insisted that we leave for the hotel. Within twenty minutes my head hit the pillow and I was out for the night. For the first time in four years, I was home. My mother and two of my grandparents were close by, and I felt somewhat safe. My stepfather no longer had total control over Emma and me. Hopefully, things would be better than they had been for the previous year.

Shortly after we returned to the United States, my grandparents took Emma and me to Oklahoma with them. Our mother and stepfather took time off together and disappeared quickly. Emma and I didn't mind at all. We were happy to be free of our stepfather. We rode home to Oklahoma with our grandparents, and bickered like normal kids the entire way. If Emma said something was black, I insisted that it was white. We drove our grandparents insane during that road trip, but we were actually able to be kids for the first time in a year. That last year in Europe, we had depended on one another to survive. We couldn't just be sisters. Once we arrived in

Oklahoma, we were reunited with our paternal grandparents. We hadn't been allowed much contact with them over the previous five years, and had been allowed absolutely no contact with them while our mother was in Pasadena and our stepfather had control. Our grandfather was battling colon cancer at the time, and we were oblivious. He could have passed away while our stepfather had control of us, and we wouldn't have been allowed to have that knowledge until we returned to the United States. Our cousins barely remembered us. Oklahoma was hot and humid like Dallas. Everyone spoke English and there weren't any random people speaking German around us. Returning to the United States was a huge culture shock for us. We attended a family reunion with our maternal grandmother and complete strangers were hugging and kissing us. After a year of never been hugged or kissed, we didn't know how to react. I'm sure that we appeared socially awkward and unloving. The truth was that I loved the attention, but I was scared that it was going to be ripped away from me. If my stepfather found out someone loved me, they would be eliminated from my life. If my family found out how worthless I was and how much my stepfather hated me, they might feel the same way too. It was nearly impossible for me to allow myself to get attached to anyone. Then Aunt Teresa and Uncle Richard walked back into my life. Or, more appropriately, I walked back into theirs. They never left Oklahoma but I did. As soon as I saw my Aunt Teresa's sweet smile and my Uncle Richard joked around with me, I knew that there was something inside of me that was worth loving.

Our grandmothers started taking Emma and I to church. There was no question about it. We were attending and we were going to like it. Our mother didn't take us to church and our last experience had been the private Catholic school. Our grandmothers attended the First Assembly of God together, along with one of our great-aunts and great-uncles. That first summer, our maternal grandmother gave each of us a Bible with a handmade fabric cover. It was the most cherished gift I had ever received. Emma set out to read hers cover to cover. I set out to find out who this amazing God was. When we were younger, our grandmothers had taken us to nursing homes on Sunday mornings to sing to the residents. I remembered that, but I didn't remember much about church itself. We attended regularly that summer, and we both accepted Jesus into our lives and our hearts as our savior. In the terms of our church, we were "saved" that summer. A new path was set for us. The God that we didn't have for the previous years of struggle was here for us now. We had the opportunity to learn about Him and grow in our faith. Emma and I both held on to that as hard as we could. The church had a wonderful youth group and we made friends with several of the kids our age. We attended cook-outs and played volleyball. We learned about how God worked in their lives. Finally, we had a big part of our lives that had been missing up to that point. Both of our grandmothers were strong in their faiths and they passed that to us. Without a doubt, that was the best gift I have ever received. Jesus Christ in my heart helped me heal from the experiences in my past and gave me strength for the obstacles I would overcome in my future. I was ready to move to Pasadena with my mother and get started on the beginning of the end of my life with my stepfather. I had four more years to go. I had survived living with him since I was three; now I had Jesus protecting me and I knew the next four years would be a breeze. Little did I know, the worst was yet to come and God was going to save me from the brink of self-destruction.

Chapter 4

Pasadena

The last year that Emma and I spent in Europe with our stepfather, our mother spent in Pasadena going to college. She was pursuing an associate's degree in fashion design. When we returned to the United States, our stepfather was stationed in Shreveport, Louisiana. Emma and I were thrilled to discover that we were going to live with our mother in Pasadena, while he finished out his military career in Shreveport. We were going to be somewhat free of him for a year! After spending the summer with our grandparents and cousins, we made our way to our new home in Pasadena. Our mother had been living in an apartment and for the first time in our lives, we had roommates. Aileen and Jeremy were students at the same college our mother attended. Aileen was also a fashion design student, and Jeremy was pursuing a degree in aviation. When we arrived, Aileen was home. She welcomed us to our new home and was excited for us to be there. There were three bedrooms in the apartment. Our mother had one, Emma and I shared one, and Aileen shared hers with Jeremy. Surprisingly, it was a spacious apartment and we settled in quickly. Jeremy came home later that day, and he had a kitten with him. The kitten's name was Mija and she was adorable. For the first time since Kindergarten, we had an animal in the house. I loved our new home and immediately felt comfortable with my new little family. Over the next few weeks, the horrors of being in Europe alone with our stepfather began to fade away into a sad memory.

I started high school shortly after we moved to Pasadena. Emma was a sophomore. Our apartment was in Deer Park's school district, so we would be attending there. Compared to our last school, Deer Park High School was huge. There were around five hundred students in the freshman class. Our mother took us to the school to enroll, and I was shocked by its size. I had no idea how I would find my way to all of my classes. How would I find Emma at lunch time? Would I make any new friends? I hadn't had to change schools since the end of third grade, and I was scared. Emma and I were expected to make B's at a minimum in school. Anything below a B would earn us a grounding until the next report card came out. I was scared that I wouldn't adjust to this new environment quickly and that my grades would suffer. That first day of school was riddled with anxiety. I received my schedule and headed toward my first class. It was Theater Arts, and classes were already in progress. The halls were empty and the silence in the hallways was deafening to me. I didn't know anyone in the class, and I was going to walk in and interrupt the class. Everyone was going to stare at me. I tried to hold off going into the class as long as possible. I walked past it five or six times before a teacher saw me and asked if I was lost. I told her I wasn't and finally mustered up the courage to walk into the classroom. All heads turned and about 30 sets of eyes looked me up and down. I was mortified. I had learned how to survive by not calling attention to myself, and suddenly I was not invisible. I managed to make it to an empty seat with my heart pounding in my ears. Fortunately, everyone turned back toward the teacher and I was forgotten.

Emma and I settled in to our new life, happy to be back with our mother and away from our stepfather. We quickly realized that we didn't fit in well at Deer Park High School. Our mother did an amazing job of finding clothes for us and trying to ensure that we had everything we needed. Since she went to college and our stepfather's income wasn't high, we qualified for reduced lunches at school. Sometimes, that was all we ate. Emma and I didn't see a problem with being on reduced lunches and were happy to go through the line and get that tray of food because we knew it would be a while before the next one. One of our friends asked why we always went through the tray line one day because there were several snack lines with tastier choices. I said something about being on reduced lunches and we were quickly ostracized. People at Deer Park had money and we didn't. They also had nice clothes and Emma and I had such a small selection that what she wore on Monday's I would wear on Friday's and such. We had about five outfits to share between us. I felt bad that we didn't fit in, but I also felt worse for my mother because I knew how hard it was to come up with the two dollars each per week that it cost to feed us at school. In Europe we had been able to buy things at the commissary and save money. We didn't have that option living in Pasadena. Aileen and Jeremy contributed as much as they could, but they were college students and low on funds as well. Despite being so poor, having only a few friends at our new school, and having little to eat, we were *happy*. For the first time since I could remember, our lives were peaceful. Some weekends our mother would go to Shreveport to visit our stepfather. We missed her but had Aileen and Jeremy there to take care of us. Life was good. We even told our mother that if she wanted to leave our stepfather, we would both get jobs to help pay bills. She didn't leave him. During that time, we scraped by the best that we could. We had to wash our clothes in the bathtub with dish detergent and hang them on the patio to dry. Usually, they didn't dry in time for school on Monday and we would have to iron our clothes to dry them. If we wanted toilet paper in the apartment, we had to steal it from public bathrooms. At one point, all we had in the house to eat was crackers and ketchup.

Emma and I would have been fine living like that forever, as long as we didn't have to put up with *him*. Unbeknownst to us, he was running up charges on a credit card that our mother didn't know anything about. He was telling her that he didn't have money to send to us, but was going out and having fun every night.

The summer between my freshman and sophomore years of high school, we were finally allowed to see our father. Our stepfather was still in Shreveport, and our mother was able to make the decision without his input. Our father had returned from an assignment to the Azores and sent us bus tickets. We boarded the bus in Houston, scared about how the visit was going to go but excited to see him. He and our stepmother had two daughters and we couldn't wait to get to know our little sisters. The bus took us from Houston to Dallas, where our father met us at the bus station. He was waiting on the sidewalk in front of the bus station when we climbed down the steps. I knew him as soon as I saw him. He was a little older, but he was the father whose face I had tried hard to remember every night before I fell asleep so I didn't forget him. Cautiously, he walked up to us. We shared a somewhat awkward hug and he asked us if we were hungry. Naturally, we were. He took us to eat at a Denny's and we were allowed to choose what we wanted. I don't think he knew how to take it when we didn't talk much. We were shy and we had grown used to not talking at the table when father figures were around. After we ate, we got into his minivan and road to our Aunt Niece's house. She was our stepmother's sister, and she immediately took us under her wing. There was a horse on her property and for the first time ever, we got to go horseback riding. Our little sisters were there. On the ride to Aunt Niece's we had asked our father if our sisters knew about us. He explained that he had just told them about us that day. They had gone their whole lives without knowing about us. We also met our cousin there. That night, we all loaded up in the minivan and headed for our father's house in Oklahoma. We got there early the next morning and were welcomed with open arms. Our stepmother was excited to see us. The entire time we were there, she would stay up late at night with us and talk to us. I believe she knew things were not good at our house. We still didn't trust anyone enough to really speak up. She took us to Sonic one day for drinks and asked us what we wanted. We were shocked that we were allowed to order something. She was shocked that we didn't know that we could actually order something ourselves. The life we were living was nothing like the life that our father, stepmother, and little sisters were living. At the end of our visit we went back to Houston, but I had finally gotten what I wanted for years. I got to see my father.

A year after we moved to Pasadena, our stepfather retired from the military. Our lives changed drastically. We moved to a new apartment away from Aileen and Jeremy. The new apartment had two bedrooms and was much smaller than our last apartment. Our furniture wouldn't fit so we had cushions in the living area to sit on and a coffee table with pillows in the dining area to eat at. There was a wooden room divider placed between the two, and Emma and I had to eat at the coffee table. When our stepfather had been in Shreveport, we were allowed to eat with the adults and actually talk during our meals. Once again, we were shunned to another area away from the adults and expected to be absolutely silent as we ate. Emma and I shared a tiny bedroom and bathroom. Quickly after we moved in, our entire apartment smelled like cigarettes again. Our mother smoked, but in moderation. The smell hadn't been an issue in the last apartment and our mother never smelled like cigarettes. Now that our stepfather was back, he brought his stink with him. Our clothes smelled like cigarettes, our hair smelled like cigarettes, and I swear even the inside of my own nose smelled like cigarettes. Just having our stepfather at the apartment made us not want to bring friends home. Now it was shabby, looked like bums lived there, and smelled disgusting. Emma and I didn't invite friends over and instead did our best to spend time with our friends.

Once he retired from the military, our stepfather descended into somewhat of a depression. He couldn't find a job. For months, he searched. He attended interviews and got numerous denial letters in the mail. He was receiving his retirement check, but funds were incredibly limited. As more time went by, he got even more depressed. The more depressed he got, the meaner he got. We had always been afraid to go home in the past when he was there. Ever since I could remember, I always got sick to my stomach as I neared whatever house we were living in, knowing he would be there. This was much worse than ever before. I would be sick during the day knowing that I had to go to that shabby, dingy, disgusting, smelly apartment after school. I knew when I opened the door, it would be something else I had to deal with. Either our room wasn't spotless or he wanted to know why one of us made an 85 on an assignment instead of a 100 or he wanted to know why supper wasn't already made. His feelings of failure were taken out on us. This was about the time that I started discovering boys. There was a handsome young man that lived in the last apartment complex that I had developed quite a crush on. I knew better than to say anything because I would never hear the end of it. One day when I was the only one home, I called the boy and talked to him. Emma and I weren't allowed to use the phone without prior permission. My stepfather found out because when he got home, he hit the redial button on the phone and the young man answered. He called me into the living room. I knew something was horribly wrong because we weren't allowed in the living room. Emma and I weren't good enough for the living room. I stood in front of him and he told me to come closer. He was sitting on a cushion. I stepped closer and he told me to come even closer. I obeyed. He got angry. He told me "I said closer!" and grabbed my arm, yanking me to the ground. In one fluid motion, he laid me over his lap, in an incredibly humiliating position. Then he proceeded to scream and cuss at me for a good fifteen minutes (I had a great view of the clock from where I was) about how disgusting I was and how he couldn't believe that I used *his* phone. He paid the bills, he bought everything in the apartment, and I had no right to use *his* phone. All I could think about was how horrible he smelled. He always had bad breath. It smelled like a skunk crawled down his throat and died. His hands always stunk. Honestly, they stunk like ass. I couldn't help but think, "Oh my God, I'm going to have to go wash my hair now because he's touching my hair and my hair's going to smell like ass." After he was done screaming and cussing at me, he hit me several times on my bottom with his bare hand. Then he pushed me off of his lap like I was a piece of garbage that disgusted him. I was a sophomore in high school at the time. Way too old to be "spanked" especially by a disgusting failure of a man that couldn't grasp the concept of good hygiene. Fortunately, karma came around and bit him a few weeks later. He was running out of money and still didn't have a job. His parents had been storing a '60-something Mustang for him and he had to sell it. The proceeds helped us get through the next couple of months before he finally found a job. Of course, Emma and I paid for his loss dearly. We were reminded constantly of how much it cost to support us and how worthless we were. I finally began to realize that he was the failure, and that he had no room to talk. Emma and I were still kids and he was the one that couldn't keep it together.

After he finally went to work and straightened his finances out, our stepfather decided that he wanted to buy a house. It looked as though for the first time ever, we would have a permanent place to live. Emma and I had made some friends and were feeling attached to the Pasadena area. My mother insisted that we look for homes in our current school district so we didn't have to change schools. We found and amazing home that had five bedrooms, two bathrooms, and a pool. Before we knew it, we were moving into our new home. Emma and I were allowed to choose colors for our bedrooms and our stepfather even painted them for us. For the first time in my life, I had a space of my own. I was sad to be away from Emma, but I realized we were getting older and needed our own space. The backyard of the home was huge and I was able to plant a vegetable garden. Finally, I had an escape like the one in my garden in Europe. I would spend hours under the hot Texas sun, planting, weeding, aerating. This time it was a vegetable garden and I couldn't wait to harvest my vegetables and feed the family. Emma and I had to take care of the pool as well. I didn't have a problem with that because I loved to swim. Unfortunately, I had angered my stepfather somehow right around the time that we moved into the house. The pool had not been taken care of by the last owners and was full of stagnant water and leaves. Instead of draining the pool and re-filling it with fresh water, my stepfather's solution was for me to remove the leaves and clean the water. I was not allowed to stand or sit on the deck to do this. I had to get into the pool, full of stagnant water, and clean it out with the net. It took me several days to clean it. Each time, I had to get into that stagnant water and try to clean out all the debris with the pool net. Once I was finally done, and chemicals were added to the water, it was clean enough for the rest of the family to get into it. I decided that I was going to enjoy every moment of that pool. I would go out at night and swim laps, enjoying some quiet time to myself with no interruptions. I watched my vegetables grow. There were many things to keep me busy. It seemed like our stepfather had backed off a little bit. We were still expected to make nothing less than a B in school. He didn't scream and cuss as much as he used to. He didn't hit us as much as he used to. It seemed he was happy at his new job and didn't have his own failures to take out on us.

Our stepfather decided that he wanted a dog. I loved the idea because I adored dogs and had wanted one for years. I was that girl that always made friends with dogs at parties and wanted several when I grew up. Someone was selling German Shepherd puppies and our mother and stepfather went to take a look. Mom had never been much of a dog lover but she didn't really have much say in the matter. Our stepfather made the point over and over that he was the one that made the money so he was the one that made the decisions. Late one evening, they came home with the cutest little ball of fur that I had ever seen. He was a white German Shepherd and we named him

Beide. That dog became my best friend. He was supposed to be our stepfather's dog, but he was definitely mine. Before we knew it, he was fully grown and absolutely huge. Beide had to spend most of his time outside and I got to the point where I spent a lot of time with him. I played with him, trained him, and loved him. Sometimes, I would get him to sleep in my room with me. Emma was working a part-time job after school by this time, so I found the companionship that I needed in Beide. He was like my baby.

Our mother did a lot of sewing. By this time, she had graduated from college with her associate's degree in fashion design. The dining room table in our home was always covered with random material, patterns, and her sewing machine. She sat down with Emma and I and taught us how to make patterns and sew our own clothes. I even made my own pattern and my own skirt one day. For some reason, our stepfather never objected to our mother's sewing, other than grumbling here and there about the mess. He had even allowed our mother to use one of the extra bedrooms as her sewing room. Her mess still made its way out to the dining room because she didn't like to be confined to one tiny room. I enjoyed that because when I was cooking supper, she and I could visit (at least until *he* got home). Unfortunately, our mother dropped some sewing needles one day and didn't realize it. Beide found them and ate them. Our stepfather had left town for a work commitment and we were home without him. Beide got very sick. He couldn't eat and just laid around. He didn't want to play and didn't even want to drink water. We took him to the veterinarian, who said to give him some Milk of Magnesia and pray for the best. Beide just got worse. I kept him in my room that night, and was up all night with him. He would settle down and go to sleep, curled up next to me. A few minutes later, he would jump up and yelp, running in circles. Nothing I did made him better. In the early hours of the morning, he began vomiting and defecating everywhere. I laid newspapers down for him because I refused to take him outside in the Texas heat in the condition he was in. This was my first experience with the "Mama Bear" feeling. I wanted to protect Beide and more than anything, I wanted to make him feel better. My stepfather got home and saw the sad condition that Beide was in. Beide was immediately taken to the emergency veterinarian. X-rays were taken and three sewing needles were discovered in his intestines. Beide had to have emergency surgery to save his life. My stepfather never protested even once. He wanted Beide to be better just as much as I did. That was the one and only time in my entire life that I saw my stepfather care about someone else more than himself. Fortunately, the needles were removed and Beide made a full recovery. I didn't care that my sister and I were screamed and cussed at for hours, or that we were grounded because we didn't find the needles before Beide did. I was just happy that my best friend in the entire world was going to live.

As I grew into a young woman, I looked more and more like my father on a daily basis. We still weren't allowed to talk openly about our father, call him our dad, or admit that we loved him. Due to looking too much like my father, my stepfather had a unique hatred for me. He thoroughly enjoyed ridiculing me for my looks, despite the fact that I was actually growing into quite an attractive young lady. My stepfather would come up with unique chores for me, reserved only for me. Yard work was one of them, which he was able to push onto me because of my love for gardening. He purchased an electric weed-eater and had a long extension cord to go with it. The extension cord was old and had some holes in it, exposing the wires beneath. This would have been an easy fix with electrical tape, but that would not have been fun for him. Instead, he would insist that I follow him around as he cut down weeds in the yard. I was expected to hold the sections of cord with exposed wires up off the ground and out of any puddles of water. It was hot and humid and I was covered in sweat within moments each time, wheezing because of my asthma, trying to fend off the mosquitoes, and hold the cord up off the ground. He would watch me closely the entire time and hurl insults and curse words my way if my hands dropped below a level that he felt was appropriate. Each time, I would try to hold back tears and just deal with the heat and mosquitoes. I would never reply to his insults, as I knew that would get me slapped. There were a few times I thought about just dropping the cord into the nearest puddle so it could electrocute us both. I just never had the courage.

Emma and I had lived in Pasadena and attended school at Deer Park long enough to have made several friends. We were never part of the popular crowd, but we did get invited to events and sleep-overs from time to time. There was a career exploration group that was sponsored by the Shell plant there, and Emma and I joined that. We went to weekly meetings and got to go on amazing field trips. Ever since I could remember, I had always wanted to be a farmer. My stepfather thought that was stupid. Emma and I weren't allowed to choose which classes we took in school, and we weren't allowed to participate in extra-curricular activities (other than the career exploration group). Athletics were out for us, despite the fact that I loved to run long distances and could swim like a fish. Our entire high school experience was, in his opinion, supposed to focus solely on academics. However, he reminded us almost daily that we were worthless and would never be good enough for anything other than breeding and being house wives. The career exploration group gave me an idea of what careers were out there. On one field trip, we went to downtown Houston and spoke to a judge in juvenile court. He had to decide whether to try a juvenile defendant as a minor or as an adult. For about forty-five minutes prior to the hearing, he spoke to our group about his career in law. We were allowed to observe the hearing from the jurors' box and I decided that I wanted to pursue a career in law. That night, I went home and told my mother. I shared how excited I was and how I planned to make the best grades ever so I could get into a good law school. My stepfather dashed those hopes when he heard about it. I believe he took great pleasure in reminding me that I was never going to be good for anything other than breeding and being a house wife.

During my junior year of high school, three amazing things happened. I was nominated for Junior Who's Who Among American High School Students, I was inducted into the National Honor Society, and I was invited to attend a week-long event for high school students at the White House. At the same time, three horrible things happened. I was not allowed to complete and submit the paperwork to be added to the Who's Who book for that year. When my family attended the National Honor Society ceremony, I was ridiculed for not being the top student of the group (there were over one hundred students inducted that night). Finally, when I received the beautiful envelope inviting me to the White House along with a schedule of events for the week, I was told that there was absolutely no way I would be allowed to go. I was expected to make amazing grades in school. When I started to receive recognition and awards for the amazing grades I made, I had to be knocked down a notch or two. My stepfather couldn't stand the idea that I might achieve something, even though he pushed me every day to do so. I was reminded that I was a disgusting failure, not worth the cost of a plane ticket to Washington D.C., and that I should never expect anything more out of life than to be a housewife that popped out a new baby every year. When it came time to take the ASVAB test to try to go into the military, which would have been a wonderful escape, Emma and I were allowed to take the test. We thought we would do well and have an opportunity to escape our home. Little did we know that he was going to prohibit us from getting our test scores. Neither of us ever found out how we did.

Many children would blame their mothers if they were treated as Emma and I were. The truth was that our mother was just as powerless as we were. She was 15 when Emma was born and 17 when I was born. Her marriage to our father didn't last and she made some poor choices after their split. She was only 19 years old at the time, with two children to take care of. For a while, she did date. Then I was beaten by her boyfriend (among other things) and removed from her custody. She fought to get me back and I firmly believe that she married our stepfather as a way to regain custody of me. The next twenty years were hell for her as well. When they married, she had been discharged from the military and did not have a high school diploma or GED. Her family was in Oklahoma and she was in South Dakota. More than anything, she wanted to get me back. She succeeded by marrying him, and I believe he reminded her of that constantly. She was 28 years old before she earned her GED. Our stepfather sent her to college and he never let her forget that he supported all of us while she was in college. She had to complete an internship before she graduated with her associate's degree. A designer took her on as an intern, and my mother had to drive over an hour each way to participate in the internship. The designer's boutique was beautiful and the designer would have helped my mother start her own career if my mother had been allowed to do so. Instead of supporting her, my stepfather constantly complained about the miles our mother was putting on the car, the amount of time she was spending away from home, and how she was not making any money. Whenever my mother mentioned getting a job, he was completely against it. When he did finally allow her to get a job, he would drive her to work and then pick her up. Our mother wasn't allowed to drive herself to work, and if he was free when she had a lunch break, she was not allowed to take her lunch break alone. He would take lunch to her and sit in the car with her while they ate. Our mother was abused and controlled just as we were. She was told constantly that she would never be anything more than a housewife. There was a stubborn streak in our mother. Many times throughout our childhood, she would be instructed to spank us for something. She would take us to another room and pretend to hit us with the belt, hitting something else instead. We would cry out as if she was hitting us. This satisfied our stepfather, as he believed she was actually spanking us as he instructed. He never bothered to observe. She would also take us on random road trips while he was at work, getting lost on purpose and making finding our way back an adventure. There were many things she did over the years to ease our suffering;

things that, had she been caught, he would have surely punished her for.

The longer Emma and I lived in Pasadena, the more friends we made. We had interests outside of the home, and our stepfather didn't like that. If we weren't in school, we were supposed to be studying, cooking, cleaning, or doing laundry. We were not supposed to enjoy our lives in any way whatsoever. If we got caught reading in our rooms and the house wasn't spotless, we would have hell to pay. It was almost impossible to keep the house spotless because everywhere you looked, our stepfather had dumped something somewhere. There was an island in the kitchen and he would pile papers and mail there. He smoked relentlessly in the living room and would rarely hit the ashtray, leaving ashes all over whatever side table he was closest to. If he had a glass in the living room, he would just leave it for us to pick up. It was hard for us to clean up after him because we weren't allowed in the living room. If we went into the living room to clean, we would get into trouble for being in there. On the flip side, if his ashtray wasn't emptied, the furniture wasn't dusted, and his tea glass wasn't picked up, we would get into trouble. At rare times, he would allow us into the living room to watch television. This usually occurred if he had friends over that he wanted to impress. Emma and I were never allowed to sit on the furniture when he was home. We weren't good enough to sit on the furniture. We had to sit on the ground. If any of his friends ever questioned it, he would tell them that we weren't good enough to sit on his furniture. Emma and I would sit there, our heads hanging down, wishing that we could be excused to go hide in our rooms but knowing that we wouldn't be. He took great pleasure in putting us down around his friends. It made him feel good to exhibit the control he had.

The worst thing that happened during my junior year in high school took place late one night, just moments after I had gotten out of the shower. Emma and I had been given our own phone line for Christmas one year. The phone was on a table in the hallway between our rooms. It had a 30-foot cord so it could reach into either room. We were constantly in trouble if the cord wasn't rolled up perfectly and tucked away behind the table. As a result, we were rarely actually allowed to use the telephone that had been a gift for Christmas. One time, our stepfather tripped over the cord and we lost it for about six months. The phone was supposed to be a gift but instead was a way to control us. I had gotten out of the shower that night and missed a call from a friend that usually gave me a ride to school. It was after 9 p.m., so I was not allowed to call him back. I took the phone into my room and locked the door, then crawled into the back of my closet and called my friend back as quietly as I could. Just seconds after I hung up and stepped out of my closet, still covered with my towel from my shower, my stepfather tried to walk into my room. We weren't allowed to lock our doors, and I had committed a cardinal sin. He began to bang on my door, screaming at me to let him in. I called out that I was changing and he said, "I don't give a flying fuck. Open this damn door right now!" As always, I obeyed. I tried to keep the towel firmly wrapped around me. The telephone had been laid quietly on the floor outside my closet. He asked me, "What the hell are you doing in here?" I explained that I had gotten out of the shower and was trying to change for bed. "Drop the damn towel, I want to make sure you're not hiding something!" he screamed at me. I tried to explain that I wasn't hiding anything and just wanted a little privacy to change. "You're a guest in this damn house, you don't get any fucking privacy," he yelled at me. "Now drop the damn towel because I know you're hiding something." Utterly humiliated, I dropped the towel. Trying to hold back tears of shame, I hung my head. He made me turn a complete circle so he could be sure I wasn't hiding something, then he proceeded to scream and cuss at me about how he was the boss in the house, I didn't belong there, and I better make damn sure I didn't disobey him. The entire time, I was not allowed to retrieve my towel or cover myself up with anything. When he was done screaming at me (and obviously had seen everything he came in there to see) he grabbed the phone and slammed the door. Naturally, I was grounded from my phone for about a month because I dared to take it into my room after 9 p.m. Never had I felt so humiliated and so vulnerable. He was the one in control over everything in that house, and I didn't even have control of my own body.

Not long after I started driver's education, my great-grandmother was killed in a motor vehicle accident. We got the call one evening, and my mother began crying uncontrollably. My stepfather took the phone, got the details about the accident and the pending funeral, and hung up the phone. My great-grandmother was a loving, kind, patient woman. She always had a smile on her face for Emma and me. Her house sat on a farm where she and my great-grandfather raised chickens. On the night of her accident, she was on the way to pick up one of my cousins. When my stepfather hung up the phone, I asked what happened. He was, of course, immediately angry. He couldn't believe that I spoke to him. How dare I address him when he didn't speak to me first? Instead of comforting me and giving me the information I needed, he chose to rant at me about how I was so rude and disgusting. Didn't I know better? Hadn't I learned after all the years of him harping on me? I should know better than to speak unless spoken to. Since I had broken one of his rules, he decided that I didn't get to know any of the details. He wasn't even sure if I was going to be allowed to go to the funeral. My mother convinced him to allow me. Fortunately, he had to work. My mother, Emma, and I, set off for the love drive to Oklahoma City. My mother wouldn't defy him and tell me what happened. It wasn't until we arrived in Oklahoma and my grandparents told me that I knew the truth behind her accident. All I had wanted to know was whether she suffered or not. Fortunately, she didn't. She had been side-swiped by another vehicle, crossed the median, and was run over by an oncoming semi-truck. Her death was instant and she suffered no pain. Due to having spoken to my stepfather first, I was not given the comfort of this knowledge until several days after my great-grandmother's death. As we stood by her grave in that little cemetery in Perry, Oklahoma, I looked at the graves of the family that passed on before me. There were many of us there. I wondered if all of them lived a life like I did, or if any of them had parents that loved them. I still believed I was worthless. My stepfather didn't even think I was good enough to know how my great-grandmother died. It was a long, quiet drive back to Houston. As always, I was sick all the way back.

As I got older, I came of age where I was able to get a job. My first job was at a fast-food restaurant, and I saved up money to buy my own car. My stepfather came across a used Chevrolet Monte Carlo. He talked to the current owners and I was not allowed to be part of the negotiation process. I was, however, allowed to go to the bank to withdraw my hard-earned money. The car was a hunk of junk and had no power whatsoever. Getting onto the busy highways in Houston was a joke. I had gone through driver's education and obtained my driver's license, but my stepfather decided he needed to teach me how to drive as well. He would take me out driving at different times. We would always take my car. I was not allowed to listen to the radio or use the air conditioner. He, of course, could do as he pleased. This included chain-smoking in my car and leaving the stench of his cigarettes and disgusting body odor behind. I never wanted to drive with him in the car, but I had no choice in the matter. One night, he decided he wanted to go out during a thunderstorm. He told me to drive about half an hour away. There was construction on the highway and the storm around us ranged. Rain was beating down on my windshield, visibility was almost non-existent, and I was scared. At one point, I somehow managed to get on a one-way road going the wrong way. Instead of trying to help me stay calm, he started to scream and curse at me. The more he screamed and cursed, the more anxious I got. I just knew we were going to die or he was going to take my car away from me. Somehow, we made it home. After that, he got worse. He wanted to take me driving all the time. One day, I did a great job driving and he made a big deal about how proud he was of me. As we pulled up in front of the house, I planned to pull into the driveway as I always did. He told me to park on the side of the road instead. I pulled up and put the car in park. "What the fuck do you think you're doing, dumbass?" he yelled at me. I was perplexed, and I'm sure the expression on my face reflected that. "You're like two feet from the curb, you stupid bitch!" he yelled at me. "Back up and pull up the right way!" I put the car in reverse, backed up, and pulled up to the curb again. What followed was about an hour of him screaming and cursing at me. "You're one stupid little retarded bitch. I can't believe they gave your stupid ass a driver's license," he yelled at one point. No matter how hard I tried, I couldn't get the car parked exactly where he wanted it. He would never tell me how close or how far he wanted the car; he just kept making me back up and pull forward while he ridiculed me for my lack of depth perception. It was over a hundred degrees that day. Still, I wasn't allowed to use the air conditioning in *my car.* Finally, after about an hour he was bored with abusing me and got out of the car, slamming the door behind him.

When children are abused, the effects of that abuse builds up in their systems in a toxic way. We can only handle so much before we break. Being a teenager is hard enough, and many times the only escape a teenager has is the safety of his or her own home. Emma and I didn't have that. School was our escape. Sometimes we could go over to friends' houses. Our stepfather instituted a rule one day that we had to request permission at least 24 hours before any social event, or we couldn't go. Teenagers do things on the spur of the moment and rarely plan ahead of time. As a result, we were left out of many social events. Our life was in that house, where we weren't wanted and where we couldn't do anything right. Around the end of my sophomore year of high school, I became involved with a young man. We fell in love and had actually talked about getting married one day. Due to always being grounded for something stupid and never being able to go anywhere, we rarely got to see each other. Naturally, the relationship broke up and I was devastated. I sank into a deep depression that even Emma couldn't get me out of. Almost daily, I thought about that young man and what could have been. I realized that my stepfather just didn't want me to have anything that might make me remotely happy, and I grew resentful. I began to hate walking through that door every day after school. Even Beide couldn't make me happy anymore, even though he tried. There was a lot of pressure at school and at home. My grades had to be perfect. The house had to be perfect. If I cooked something my stepfather didn't like, he would spit it out in the trash and then hand me his plate for me to eat it. The yard had to be perfect. All I wanted to do was curl up in a little ball and cry until my broken heart mended a little bit. I didn't have that opportunity. While many young girls my age could curl up in their mothers' arms and cry, I didn't have that luxury. My mother was not accessible to me. She was stuck in the living room with him and I was too busy trying to be perfect. Emma was working and trying to enjoy her senior year of high school. There was not a person in this world that I could talk to. My depression grew worse and I began to consider suicide. If I wasn't even welcome in my own home, why would I think anyone else would want me in their lives? Along came my friend, Amanda. She realized there was a sadness inside of me that hadn't been there before. Although she tried to get me to talk to her, I wouldn't. I hit rock bottom the night that I stood in the bathroom holding a razor blade, ready to take my own life. That night, God intervened and put a spark of fighter in me that was never there before. That spark has since grown into a flame and I have not backed down from a fight my entire adult life. But back then, that little spark was what kept me on this earth. After God and I had our talk that night, I had a long talk with Amanda.

Amanda and I had been friends since sophomore year. Her parents had gone through a messy divorce and she was living in a camper with her dad for a long time. She and I were close because while I was battling my own demons, she was battling hers. The difference between me and Amanda was that she had two parents that loved her dearly. They helped her through all of her challenges, and she knew that she was loved. I envied that and wished that I could be as good as Amanda so that someone would love me too. Although Amanda and I were close, I never told her that I almost killed myself. I also never told her how God intervened. Instead, I just told her that I was ready to escape. By this time, I had been allowed to start working. I had saved up enough money to purchase my own car. I even paid for the insurance myself. My mother and stepfather were planning a weekend away from home, and I felt that was the perfect opportunity for me to leave. Some friends went with me to get my own insurance (I paid for my policy on my stepfather's plan) and I began to discreetly pack things. I didn't have much. The night before I left, I wrote a letter to my mother. In the letter, I laid everything out to her that was in my heart. I explained that I loved her, but I couldn't be in that house anymore. I told her that I knew they didn't love me or want me and that I was just a burden. I told her that I was all alone trying to mend my broken heart, and that instead of anyone there helping me, they just piled on more for me to do. Although I never told her that I almost committed suicide, I did tell her that I didn't want to be on this earth anymore if it meant living with my stepfather. I explained that I had been beaten, screamed at, cussed at, and ridiculed to the point that I had no desire to be a part of their lives and I was leaving. The next day, Amanda and her father came to get me. We moved all of my belongings out of the house while no one was home and I left the letter for my mother. As we drove off, I didn't look back even once. I thought I was finally free.

That weekend was the best weekend of my life. For the first time, I had not a care in the world. My stepfather wasn't waiting for me at home, ready to scream at me or hit me simply for existing. Amanda's father didn't care if I made good grades, he only cared that I went to school and passed. I visited friends that I hadn't seen in a long time, went grocery shopping with Amanda, and even put on fake fingernails that I was prohibited from wearing in the past. I truly believed that once my mother read my letter and realized how depressed I was, she would leave me alone. Sunday came, and Amanda and I went to a friend's house. We sat in the driveway and visited with our friend, not causing any trouble. My mother and stepfather drove up and parked behind us, blocking my car in. Instead of getting out of the car, my stepfather remained in the driver's seat. Out came my mother, angrier than I have ever seen her. She told Amanda to get out of the car and made me slide over. I had never disobeyed her in my entire life, and I was scared out of my mind. She got in the driver's seat and took off. That was the last time I ever saw Amanda or her friend. As we drove home, my mother was the one that did the screaming and cussing. I didn't have a chance to say anything. Desperately, I tried to peel the fake fingernails off, knowing that I was going to get into trouble for those too. We got to the house and I was ordered inside. Then I was told to pick up the phone and call my father. I looked at my mother, completely perplexed. "Call your damn father and beg him to live with him. You don't live here anymore," she snarled at me. I picked up the phone and dialed the number, praying that he answered. He did. I told him what I did and he told me to come to Oklahoma, and that I was more than welcome to stay with him. After I hung up the phone, my mother began screaming at me. I asked her if she read my letter. She said that she did, and that she didn't give a "flying fuck" how I felt. My feelings didn't matter. Since I didn't want to be there, I could just go stay with my father. I was an ungrateful piece of shit. That was about the time my stepfather walked into the house. He was holding the distributor cap from my car. The car that I had worked for and paid for. I was told that my car was being taken from me. I didn't know what to do or say, and instead went to my room and waited for the inevitable.

That night, I didn't sleep at all. I cried and worried about the future. I hadn't lived with my father, and now my mother was sending me to the home of someone she hated that she had told me my whole life didn't want me. My car was being taken from me, even though I worked for it and the title was in my name. That's when I decided that my stepfather wasn't getting the car that I paid for. I went into the living room about 3 a.m. and found the title in the desk, along with an envelope and a stamp. The title went into the envelope with my signature on the back, and was addressed to a long-time friend of mine. I hid the envelope in my room, praying that they wouldn't discover that the title was missing. The next day, we were bound for Oklahoma. For hours I sat in the back of that car, watching my life in Pasadena shrink more and more behind me. I wasn't allowed to speak on the entire trip, and my mother and stepfather took every opportunity to remind me how ungrateful and worthless I was. When we arrived in Oklahoma, I expected the same reception from my father and stepmother. They were quiet as we all sat in the living room, going over the plan for me. My mother wanted me to go to counseling and also wanted me to have a pregnancy test (because I had been such a whore that I slept with the young man I had fallen in love with). Every detail about my life was spread out on the table, and not a single person asked me if I was okay. Then my mother left me there, like I was a piece of trash she was happy to be rid of. I didn't realize that she was hurting too, and doubting her decision. All I knew was that she left me with the one person that she hated more than anything in the world. Never in my life did I feel so hurt and alone. I watched her ride away in the car with my stepfather and realized that she chose him over me. I thought that she would always choose him over me. Now, even worse, she left me with her worst enemy because I had rebelled and ran away.

When I stayed in Oklahoma, I got to spend time with my father and stepmother. I had two younger sisters that I barely knew. My grandparents were close by and I got to spend time with them. None of them said a word about what happened in Pasadena. They didn't harp on me every minute of every day. There were rules that I needed to follow, but I wasn't put down or ridiculed if I made a mistake. I spent time with my little sisters and realized they were being raised much differently from myself. They actually got to be kids. My father took time to take me places alone and would try to talk to me. My stepmother got angry one day when my mother called and upset me by bringing up the fact that I ran away. My father and stepmother were on my side. I still didn't trust them, though. I kept myself shut off from them even though I wanted desperately to confide in them. More than anything, I wanted to stay there and live with them. Still, I was deceitful. I took the envelope with the title to my car and mailed it to my friend in Houston. That way, the car belonged to him and my stepfather couldn't take it away. I used the telephone at my grandmother's house to call my friends and tell them that I was okay. Unfortunately, that got back to my mother when a friend left a message on Emma's answering machine saying that she had talked to me. They discovered that the title to my car was missing and all hell broke loose. My mother was incredibly angry and made sure I knew it from hours away. Instead of becoming angry, my father tried to sit down and talk to me. He tried to find out what was really going on with me. By then, I had already learned that I was worthless and no one loved me. It didn't make any sense to confide in him, because my truth wasn't worth listening to. He asked me to stay with him. Even though that was the one thing that I wanted in the world, I couldn't bring myself to agree. I couldn't leave my mother alone in that house with that monster, and I couldn't trust my father when he said he loved me. Emma was the only person in the whole world that loved me, and if I stayed in Oklahoma I wouldn't see her anymore. Ultimately, I made the choice to return to my mother's home because I didn't want her to have to deal with my stepfather alone. Too many adults in my life had turned their backs on me when I needed them, and I believed it would just be a matter of time before my father did, too. Also, my car was in Houston and my stepfather told me the only way I would get it back was if I graduated from high school there. My father told me he would buy me a car himself, but I didn't trust him enough to see if he would actually do it.

Chapter 5

Amarillo

I started my senior year of high school in Deer Park. There was a determination inside of me that would not fail. I would graduate with my friends and I would get my precious car back. Many of my friends hadn't seen me since the school year before. After I ran away, I was forced to quit my job. Aileen had a friend that ran a printing shop and I was put to work there. It was a job that I loved immediately, and the boss loved me. My stepfather unexpectedly quit his job because of a dispute over safety glasses. At the time, my mother was allowed to work at Dillard's. We had her income and his military retirement. He talked my boss into letting him work at the printing shop in the afternoons. Each day, he would pick me up from school and we would drive about forty-five minutes to the printing shop. We would work for a few hours and go home. When my stepfather realized that I loved the job and that the people there liked me, he had to put a stop to it. Instead of looking for jobs in the Houston area, he began to look for jobs all over the state of Texas. One afternoon I was completely devastated when I came home from school and he greeted me in the kitchen. He had a huge smile on his face and said he had found a job. I asked him where his job was. He told me it was in Amarillo. I had never even heard of Amarillo so I asked where that was. He said it was in the panhandle of Texas, about two hours away from my hometown. I thought he was taunting me and didn't believe him at first. He went on to say that we would be moving there within the next two weeks, and that I could kiss my life in Houston goodbye because it was over. That's when I realized he wasn't joking. He had found a job as far away as he could in Texas and was moving me there because he knew I wanted to finish school with my friends in Deer Park. At this point, I was still grounded for running away. The plan was that I would remain grounded until I graduated from high school. Once I graduated I could have my car back and move out. Now, I would never see my friends again. Not even in school.

The next two weeks were a blur. My mother was sad for me and tried to make things better. We took a trip to

Amarillo and she told me that I could choose any school that I wanted there. Over the weekend, we drove all over Amarillo. We even drove to Panhandle and looked at the school there. On the way back, we passed by Highland Park. It was just outside of Amarillo, in the country. There was an old Air Force base that had been shut down. A private company had purchased the housing and converted it into rental properties. Highland Park reminded me of the school I attended in Oklahoma right before we moved to Europe. That's where I wanted to be. We stopped at the housing office, toured a house, and my mother put a deposit down that day. Moving to Amarillo was a reality now, but I had won a small victory by being allowed to choose my school. We returned to Houston and I made the best of the time that I had left with my friends. I found an old rotary phone in the garage and used it in my bedroom late at night to call friends. The last night we were in Houston, I called the young man that I had been in love with. We talked for hours and I wished him the best. I knew I would most likely never see him again. For the rest of the night, I did nothing but cry. I was having to pick up and move yet again, during the year that was supposed to be the best year of high school for me. It was unfair and it hurt my heart. By the next morning, my head was splitting and all of my teeth hurt. I knew better than to ask for pain medication of any kind. Instead, I climbed into my mother's car with her and began the long drive to Amarillo. My stepfather was driving a U-Haul truck, had Beide in the cab with him, and was pulling my car behind it. We followed closely behind him. As we drove out of Houston, my mother confided that she didn't want to move to Amarillo. She was leaving friends behind as well, and felt that her husband was making us move because we had friends in Pasadena and we were happy. About an hour into our drive, we saw a sign that said "Houston" and pointed to the turn-around on the highway. I told my mother that we could turn around right there and go back. We could live with Aileen and start a new life. I believe she pondered it for a moment, but continued to follow my stepfather.

We drove all the way to Amarillo that day, and the trip was anything but boring. At one point, we stopped at a rest stop to use the bathroom and walk Beide. I was standing by the truck with Beide and my stepfather walked out of the bathroom about 100 feet away. He called to Beide, who immediately went running toward him. Beide was on a leash, which was wrapped around my wrist. I weighed a whopping 98 pounds at the time and was no match for the fully grown and overly-excited German Shepherd. Despite my pleas to Beide to stop, my stepfather kept calling him and I was stuck running behind him. I couldn't free my wrist from the leash, and I couldn't keep up with Beide. Down I went, and my stepfather kept calling Beide. As Beide continued to run, I was dragged behind him. I was on my back, my wrist caught in the leash, being dragged across sticks and rocks. By the time Beide reached his destination, my entire back was scraped badly. Instead of saying that he was sorry, my stepfather sneered at me and told me if I wasn't such a fat-assed idiot, I would have been able to run with Beide. My stepfather had learned years before in

Europe that I loved to run distances. He put a stop to my running. Now that I was out of shape because I wasn't allowed to run, he was holding it against me. I climbed back into my mother's car and tried to keep my back from touching the seat the rest of the way to Amarillo. We didn't stop for peroxide or bandages. I didn't have the opportunity to clean my back. I just had to suffer through it. My head and teeth still hurt, and now my back and pride hurt as well. My mother was angry about this, and was also angry that we hadn't eaten yet. About an hour later, my stepfather stopped for gas. We got gas and my mother asked when we were going to eat. He didn't give her an answer. We parked the car as he went inside to pay for the gas. When he came out, he was holding a box of chicken. It was a box for one person. My mother wasn't allowed to carry money and he knew she didn't have money to feed me or herself. He walked up to the car, holding the box of chicken in one hand and munching on a piece of chicken with the other. He leaned into the car through my window to speak to my mother and she blew up. Within seconds, they were screaming and cursing at one another with me stuck in the middle. I had nowhere to go. Every time he would scream at her, he would end up spitting on me and spewing his ass-breath saliva all over me. I was trying not to cry and not to gag all at once. Finally, he threw the box of chicken in my lap and stomped off to the truck. He left the parking lot and once again, my mother followed behind him. We drove for about an hour before I had the courage to utter a word. I had a box of chicken in my lap and we were both hungry. The first thing I said was, "How mad do you think he would be if we ate his chicken?" My mother burst out laughing and said that it would serve the bastard right. We ate that box of chicken and enjoyed every bite of it. About an hour after that, he stopped at a restaurant. He had finally decided to feed us. He was not happy that we had eaten his chicken but my mother told him she really didn't care. That was the first time I had ever seen my mother rebel against her husband.

We arrived in Amarillo late that night. My grandparents met us there and helped us unload the U-Haul. I went to bed at around two that morning and was up for school the next day. My mother went with me to register and all eyes were on us as soon as we walked in. Highland Park was a small school. I was hoping this would help me make friends quickly. We spoke to the counselor and I was given a schedule. Instead of walking alone to my first class, the counselor walked with me. It was my English class. We walked in the door and everyone turned around and stared. The teacher was about 23 years old and very pretty. She had a huge smile on her face and introduced me to the class. One of the students said that when everyone saw me that morning, they thought I was a freshman. I only stood 5'1" and weighed less than a hundred pounds. I found a seat and quickly realized that, although I was being stared at, they weren't unfriendly stares. The teacher announced that we would be working in groups that morning. I didn't know anyone and was immediately afraid I would be left out. A pretty blonde-headed girl got up and walked over to me. She invited me to join her group, which I readily accepted. Another girl was in that group. She was a pretty brunette girl with friendly eyes.

Immediately, she took me under her wing. She invited me to sit with her at lunch, and I readily accepted. Throughout my day, I quickly discovered that the majority of the students at Highland Park were friendly. They were all amazed that I was a senior, but were happy to accept me into their groups. There was never a day at Highland Park that I worried about where I would sit or if I would fit in. My savior from the first day of school introduced me to people outside of school as well, which was how I met my lifelong best friend. I loved Highland Park from that very first day.

Despite the friendliness I encountered at Highland Park, I was still somewhat socially awkward. I never initiated a conversation because I didn't know how. For years I had been told not to speak unless I was spoken to. At Deer Park, I could hide in the shadows and enjoy some anonymity. At Highland Park, that just wasn't possible. Some classmates felt I was a bit of a snob, but they didn't know what I had been through or what my life at home was like. I was painfully quiet even at school. Not long after we moved to Amarillo, I found a job. Between work and school, I was rarely home. My stepfather worked nights, so when I was at school, he was sleeping. When I was at work, he was getting ready for work. For the most part, the beginning of my life in Amarillo was peaceful. I was allowed to drive my car, but I was reminded constantly that I had to graduate to be able to keep it. I dated one young man briefly, but that didn't last long. Then one day, a friend came to my locker and told me that someone else liked me. His name was Steven and he was a close friend of the young man I had dated. We began dating and from that moment on, I didn't have eyes for anyone else.

One day early on in our relationship, I was speaking to Steven on the phone. We were planning a date and joking around. My mother became involved in the conversation and the three of us were joking around with one another. My stepfather walked into the room and without saying a word, he walked over, yanked the receiver out of my hand, and hung up the phone. I looked at him with a perplexed look, as did my mother. He told me that he didn't care who I thought I was, that I would never speak disrespectfully to my mother again. My mother tried to explain that the three of us were joking, but he wouldn't hear it. I was not allowed to call Steven back, and had to wait until the next day at school to explain. As I told him what had occurred the night before, he listened to me intently. Something told me that I could share my story with him, so I told him how my stepfather was. I told him about many of the things that had occurred since I was three. The more I talked, the angrier Steven got. For the rest of the school year, he did his best to protect me. His home became the one that I hid out at when I didn't want to go home. There were many times that I got off work early and went to his house. His mother sat in the living room with us and talked to us. She cooked for us and joked around with us. Many times, she tried to joke around with me and I didn't understand her humor. Steven took her to the side one day and explained to her what kind of life I was living at home. After that, she didn't try to joke around as much and instead tried to be gentle and understanding. Finally, the day of my high school graduation came. I couldn't believe I had made it. I was third in my class. Of course, my stepfather wanted to know why I wasn't valedictorian. I was happy with being third out of thirty-six students, and was happy to walk across the stage to get my diploma. The very next morning, I moved out of that house. I had already packed everything I owned. I got the title to my car and moved into Steven's house with him and his parents. I had my own room and began the healing process. That day was the first day of the rest of my life. I had survived. I was free.

Chapter 6

Emma's Memories

Emma experienced things that I knew nothing about. With her permission, I am writing this chapter about some of the things that she went through alone. She and I relied heavily on one another. Most of our experiences, we went through together. Emma was the one shining light in my life that kept me going. Late at night we would whisper to one another about our fears, hopes, and dreams. We would imagine what it would be like when we were away from our home, living lives of our own. Both of us wanted children, but we were scared of what kinds of mothers we would be. We didn't want our children to have a stepfather like ours. Despite sharing many of our deepest secrets, and going through most of our pain together, there were some things that we experienced apart from one another. Until I started writing this book, I didn't know the things I'm about to write for her. Emma didn't know many of the things that I wrote about, until she read the rough draft. Together, we have found some healing in writing this book together. This is her story.

When Emma was about four or five years old, we lived in the little pink house in South Dakota. Our stepfather was a military recruiter at the time. Most of our time was spent playing in the basement in that house and trying to remain invisible. Emma suffered from sinus problems, and while she slept one night, her nose began to bleed. The next morning when she awoke, her nose was crusted over with blood. Our stepfather saw it, and became incredibly angry with her. In his mind, he decided that she had picked her nose and made it bleed. Picking one's nose, as Emma soon discovered, was a serious offense. Emma was still in her little nightgown, and our stepfather had come parading out of his room in his underwear.

I guess he thought he had something magical to show off or found himself attractive. In reality, he was disgusting and needed to invest in a thick robe that covered him from head to toe. He saw Emma's little nose and instead of helping her clean it up and giving her some medicine for her sinus problems, he began to scream at her. He couldn't believe she would be so disgusting that she would pick her nose. He picked her up and carried her to the bathroom. When they got to the bathroom, he shoved her face into the mirror and showed her how her nose looked. As he stood there, holding her up to the mirror, he ridiculed her for her appearance. He was still in only his underwear, with his disgusting body pressed against her tiny little form. Emma was humiliated, uncomfortable, and disgusted. He had to show her how completely he was in control of her every move, including how she conducted herself while sleeping. What a big, bad man it took to push his disgusting body up against a four year old child to show her how much control he had.

Around the same time, while we still lived in the pink house, he became angry with Emma for something. She still doesn't know why he was angry. All she remembers is that she was sitting at the table working on homework or coloring. She had paper and was working hard on whatever it was. Our stepfather walked into the room and saw her at the table. Without saying a word or providing any explanation of any kind, he walked over to her and slammed his fist down onto her finger. Her tiny little finger was smashed between his fist and the table. Our mother came into the room and Emma was crying. Somehow, he convinced our mother that it was an accident. By that time, Emma knew better than to speak up. She remained silent as our mother doctored her tiny little smashed finger.

While living in Europe, a lady came to talk to Emma's class. The lady talked to the whole class about child abuse. She explained what it was and encouraged any child in the class that was being abused or knew someone that was being abused to go to a teacher and tell them. The teacher could help, and make sure the child was safe. Emma sat there listening in class, feeling sorry for the poor abused children. How could parents do that to children? She wanted to help anyone that was being abused. If she heard of that happening, she would be sure to help any way that she could. It never occurred to Emma that *she* was the abused child. She never spoke up because the life that we were living at the time was all she knew. Emma didn't realize that our life was not normal. We weren't allowed to talk about what occurred at home, but that didn't send up any red flags. We had never been allowed to. Ever since we could remember, our reality had been living the life we lived with our stepfather. We didn't know anything else. We certainly didn't know it wasn't normal. Had that woman given an example, perhaps it would have helped Emma. Instead, she simply said that kids were being abused and needed help. We were so close to help, yet so far away. The lack of an example held back the help that we desperately needed.

One memory that Emma and I share, that we both agree on, was that our mother was a victim, too. We never held any sort of grudge against her, and we did everything we could to protect her. Had the need arose, we would have protected her with our lives. We are in complete agreement that she would have done the same for us. Our mother was a young mother with no resources of her own, doing the best that she could. Emma and I love her dearly and remember many amazing times with her. She did the best that she could with what she had. Instead of loving her and cherishing her as he should, our stepfather bullied, manipulated, and controlled her. Our beautiful mother was not allowed to work, not allowed to have friends that weren't approved by him, not allowed to be a part of the budgeting and bill-paying process, and certainly never allowed to carry money of her own.

Emma suffered at the hands of our stepfather just as I did. She was scared to become a mother because of the fear of continuing the cycle of abuse. When her first baby was born, my first baby was two weeks old. Emma and I had always done everything together, so naturally, we became mothers together. Every bad thing that had happened to us, we both used for good when it came to our own children. We both swore that we would raise our children opposite of how our stepfather raised us. If we followed that path, our children would be happy. We both stuck to it. Emma has other memories of things that our stepfather did; these memories are her story to tell and not mine. I have shared a few of the things I felt needed to be added to this book with her blessing. Thankfully, Emma and I both survived. Her heart has healed, too.

Epilogue

Katie Grimsley, the little girl from Oklahoma who endured years of abuse at the hands of her stepfather no longer exists. Emma Grimsley doesn't exist anymore, either. In their places are two grown women in their early forties. Katie has four beautiful children, three amazing dogs, and lives with her best friend who is a combat veteran and works in the law enforcement field. She is a grandmother to two adorable children. Emma is married with two beautiful children and a husband who retired from the Air Force this past year. Both have succeeded in working, raising a family, and pursuing college educations. Katie is currently pursuing her first master's degree while Emma is currently pursuing her doctorate. They are closer than most sisters, despite having taken two completely different paths after graduating from high school. Katie has lived in the same town since her senior year of high school while Emma married an Air Force man and traveled the world. Neither time nor distance could break the bond that formed between them. They endured things together that no children should ever have to. Not only did they endure them, but they came out of their experiences on top. All of their children are happy, abundantly-loved, well-adjusted individuals. They all want to spend time with their families. When Katie and Emma set about their adult lives and became mothers, all they ever wanted was to raise children that wanted to be a part of their lives when they were older. Katie and Emma succeeded, and they did that while juggling careers and pursuing their educations. Katie did marry and divorce, but her ex-husband and the father of their children remains one of her closest friends. He remarried and Katie's children have an amazing extra mom who adores them. Everyone gets along and they even spend holidays and weekends camping together. Katie will never remarry and is instead content in sharing a life with her best friend and helping him raise his children. Katie's children and grandchildren never worry about tension between their parents because it doesn't exist. Katie is gone and in her place is that happy, confident, successful woman that escorted her son, along with his other two parents, out of that inflatable tunnel and onto the football field.

REPORTING ABUSE AND/OR NEGLECT

If you, or someone you know, is being abused or neglected *please make a report.* Each state has a system to receive these reports and respond to them. Website links have been included below; one for the Child Welfare Information Gateway and the other for the Texas Department of Family and Protective Services (for readers that reside in Texas). When children are being abused or neglected, our silence and lack of action mean those children won't get the help that they desperately need. Even if you only suspect abuse or neglect, please report it. Don't turn a blind eye to a child that needs help. So many people turned blind eyes when Katie and Emma were living in a daily hell. Years later, Katie's nephew lost his life as a result of child abuse. Please protect these children. They are our future and they need us.

Child Welfare Information Gateway
https://www.childwelfare.gov/topics/responding/reporting/
800-394-3366

Texas Department of Family and Protective Services
http://www.dfps.state.tx.us/Contact_Us/report_abuse.asp
800-252-5400

You can always call your local police station or law enforcement agency, local welfare agency, or even dial 9-1-1 if you are in immediate danger. If you're in school, talk to a counselor, the nurse, a teacher, or another adult. At church you can talk to your pastor or another adult you feel comfortable with. Talk to someone, and let them know you or someone else needs help.

Made in United States
North Haven, CT
25 October 2023